COACHING CHILDREN IN SPORT

A book to build your 'Coaching World'

By Paul Kilgannon

CONTENTS

DEDICATION

This book is dedicated to the memory of my late father Tony Kilgannon. He was a good and honest man who worked hard all his life. He was a Carpenter, a self-taught student of excellence and a true master of his craft until the very end. My hope is that I can be true to many of his good qualities and gain satisfaction through following my passion. Lessons in excellence can be taken from every walk of life.

THANKS

To my Family- Dad (RIP), Mam, Susie and Simon.

To my comrades in Carnmore Hurling Club. Viva la Reds forever!

To Anthony Watson- My lifelong best friend and sounding board.

To Mike Fox and Fergal McEvoy- Two men who have loyally stood with me through the toughest times in my coaching career.

To my old and dear friends- There is never enough time to spend together but we are always tight.

For listening and giving me their time and feedback on this project; Paul Kelly, Damien Joyce, Richard Boles, David Morris, Sinead O'Sullivan, Paul Kinnerk, Wade Gilbert, Christy O'Connor, Joe Carney, Sharon Byrne, Mark Finlay, Donie Fox, Kevin Moran, Keith Duggan, Tony Og Regan, Gary Sice, Fran Keenan, Kathleen Gilgannon, Niall O'Toole, Paudie Butler, Kevin Keane, Nick Hill and Alan Moran.

To Niall at TheDocCheck.Com for backing the project, working hard, bringing energy and making it happen.

To James Joyce and Michael Coyle in Concordi for the graphics.

FOREWORD

This book is my effort at having an influence on the lives of volunteer sports child coaches and children in sport. I am just an 'ordinary' coach if such a thing exists. I haven't coached world champions or superstars. This is a book for coaches who want to make a positive difference to the lives of children, enjoy their coaching and develop as a coach. It is my hope that the book will inspire and assist volunteer child coaches to gain a fuller perspective on their role, realise its vast potential, educate themselves and practice, self- improvement, learning and excellence in coaching children. This is fundamentally a book about learning and practice. For me, continuous learning is the job, and indeed the art, of coaching. To survive and thrive, the coach must continue to learn.

I've been involved in coaching all my adult life. Hurling is my first love, but I have coached many other sports and physical activities. I am also a Primary School Teacher by profession for 13 years now. I see coaching and teaching as one and the same, and gleam much of my knowledge, insights and beliefs from both. What I learn in coaching I use in the classroom, and what I learn in the classroom I use in my coaching. In reality, coaching and teaching are one.

I enjoy observing, and assisting, improvement and learning. I am also intrigued by the power and potential of the collective. I believe in the power of common sense. I enjoy and gain much from science and research but generally come to my own conclusions. Fads come and go and the latest trend will bring up new concepts but the basics will always be the basics and mastering these will always lead to better performance both in playing and coaching. All too often I see coaches looking outward when they may be much better served looking inwards.

"Adapt what is useful, reject what is useless, and add what is specifically your own."
Bruce Lee- Martial Artist

I was probably 15 years old when I first got involved in working with children in local summer camps. I'm unsure if I was any good, but whether I was or not is of little importance as I am a believer in the power of diligence and continuous learning. A vocation is something we grow into. From there I went on to coach at every level within my local club, Carnmore Hurling Club, literally, from U-6 to senior level. I have been involved with pretty much every age group at one time or another. I became coach of our adult Senior Hurling Team at the age of twenty-six. Prior to this I had coached exclusively at child and youth level. Together, the team went on a journey. We won no cups or trophies but we came somewhere close to achieving our true potential. That, to me, is success.

Throughout those three years I learned lots and made many mistakes. It was definitely a tough education. The players I was trying to coach were so 'adapted' or fixed into their patterns, behaviours and practises. They had many ingrained bad habits and changing something that has been adapted over time is really tough. This is why child coaching is so important. Through developmental child coaching, we can help make the player adaptable, resilient and intelligent. The challenge of adult coaching is that by the time you get them, many are just so stuck in their practices. Adaptability to change is a key element in sporting performance.

After three years coaching our senior hurling team, I took a little time out from sports coaching and planned a career break from teaching. I dreamed of getting involved in some type of professional sports coaching somewhere in the world. During this period, I spent my time studying and researching exercise, sport and coaching. As is often the case, life's events got in the way and I found myself back teaching (I never actually left teaching) and coaching children.

The pressure of 'success' or 'winning' was always something that taxed me when I was originally involved in adult coaching. I took defeat hard because I always felt responsible for the team, and I suppose, carried the responsibility of coach heavily. So at the time, leaving adult coaching was a relief. It was probably down to not understanding my role. In retrospect, I was a good 'trainer' in many ways, but I was definitely not a good coach (we will look at this distinction shortly). I hadn't fully developed my own 'Coaching Philosophies', my framework for coaching improvement. My limited and limiting perspective on my role made it impossible for me to really enjoy it, and limited my potential to flourish as a coach.

I have always been one for reading and researching, and somehow seem to find my way into things before they come into the universal consciousness of those around me. My interest in coaching, both the collective and the individual, continued to both inspire me and haunt me throughout my twenties and probably to this day. I have always wanted to know more and do better.

Shortly after finishing coaching my own senior club (and my proposed career break cancelled), I returned to child coaching and began to really enjoy it. I actually did it away from the team sporting environment at first and coached children, with learning and physical disabilities, exercise to improve their physical, social and emotional health. In this non-competitive, non-sporting environment my awareness of the power, potential and scope of coaching became acute. I began to look at coaching from a different perspective. It was a noble pursuit when I practiced it nobly. I got a true appreciation for what coaching actually is and I found I was pretty good at it.

As always, the inquisitive side of me was wondering; *How can I do this better? What is best practice?* This time the 'pressure of winning' was off. My perspective was different. I had new 'lenses'. These were clear and so it became increasingly obvious that the area of child coach was an area I had huge knowledge and interest in. I knew much of what I needed to know. I just had to effectively join the dots, make the connections and come up with a clear and cohesive philosophy for my coaching, my own way of looking at it and my own framework for continuous improvement.

As I became increasingly aware of the power of the child coach, my coaching improved and I returned to child sports coaching at club level. In my opinion, I returned to child sports coaching a far superior coach than when I left it. In truth I feel I left a 'trainer' and returned a 'coach'. I returned with a clear philosophy, a set of values and guiding principles, a brand new way of looking at things and a means of holding myself accountable to this new world.

Good coaching is good coaching, and I believe although this book is written for the child coach, there is much in it for both the teen and adult coach. The principles hold strong. Indeed, many of my beliefs and insights have come from the challenges of coaching adults and gaining an understanding of the most important qualities an adult player needs to succeed and reach their potential. I have recently finished coaching and managing an adult senior football team whom I spent three years with. For me, adult coaching is much tougher than child coaching. Again, it's the 'adapted' nature of the adult that is the most challenging. This really cements my beliefs in how important child coaching is and how much scope there is for improvement in coaching practices.

Over the past few years, through opportunities afforded to me, I have been compelled to begin collating my coaching thoughts, ideas and philosophies into presentations, workshops, manuals and models on child and teen coaching in sport and club coaching structures. These endeavours have seen me drill down into the essence of coaching. My challenge has been; how do you coach a coach to be a coach? and this book is the natural progression from that. Through working with volunteer coaches in voluntary sports clubs, I have quickly come to the conclusion that there really is such a need for volunteer coach education and mentoring in sport. Coaching is a craft, and yet I feel society grossly underestimates it and undervalues it. I genuinely think effective child and teen sport coach education can markedly improve the world. I believe youth coaching in sport is a powerful tool to deal with many and most of our social ills; obesity, mental health problems, substance abuse, bullying, and so on. According to the National Alliance for Youth Sports (NAYS), approximately 65% of children worldwide are involved in sports activities. If volunteer coaches and clubs can provide a healthy sporting environment that consciously develops the physical, social and emotional wellbeing of the child, how big a societal difference can we make? For me, coach education is the only way to do this.

I want this book to be relatively light, easy reading, thought provoking and useful. It is not designed to be a text book, rather a genuine catalyst and aid for learning and personal development in coaching. I want it to be an agent for change. I see it as a book you might read, and then return to it and reread again and again, and get something new from it each time. I want it to be simple and practical, yet comprehensive. I don't really want to tell you what to; see, think or do. I just want to teach you to; look, see, think, plan, do and then assess your doing. I want to give you the tools or a framework to allow you to build your own 'Coaching World' and then to continually improve that world through on- going learning.

Finally, I want this book to make sense. It is not overtly about science or research, although I have included what I believe is an appropriate amount of that material in it. It's about using knowledge, honouring common sense and changing perspective. As you read, continually ask yourself, *DOES THIS MAKE SENSE*? If it doesn't make sense it is useless, and if it does, it is useful. Simple as that. I believe this is a book worth writing and I hope it is a book you deem worthy of reading and using in your coaching life.

That's my story,

Paul Kilgannon

PLEASE NOTE
IMPORTANT INFORMATION

For the purpose of this book perhaps the simplest and most useful way is to categorise children in sport as **'younger children' 5-8 years and 'older children' 9 to 12 years**. Granted this is a fairly broad scope and chronological age isn't necessarily an accurate means to judge a child but for now we will use it as a working model. I will cover the age appropriate differences as much as I feel necessary, and advise you to books and other sources I believe will be beneficial to help you continue to develop as a coach. I feel lots of this more specific age appropriate information can be accessed, should you have the required interest and discipline to do so.

This book is for the **coaches of team invasion sports**. Team invasion sports are those that are characterised by the objective of invading the opponent's territory with the ultimate goal of scoring points. They have similar play principles and many transferable skills. Examples of team invasion sports include; Soccer, Hurling, Gaelic football, Rugby, Basketball, Hockey, Handball etc.

CHAPTER 1
WHAT IS COACHING
IN CHILD SPORT?

Let us begin with what, for me, is the most obvious question, what is coaching in sport? My next question is, have you thought about this deeply enough, if at all? I'm assuming by choosing to read this book you must have some interest in coaching, so you must appreciate the importance of having a clear understanding of what it actually is. I believe many potentially good coaches actually haven't taken sufficient time to do so. I don't blame them for this, or look down on them, because the vast majority of coaches are volunteers who have full time jobs outside of coaching. However, I am sure you can appreciate the tragedy in this.

For me, one thing coaching definitely is not, is our conventional understanding of 'training' or being a 'trainer'. A 'trainer' is not a coach. Before I go any further, if you are currently what I call a 'trainer', this doesn't make you a bad person. We all have a 'trainer' in us somewhere and many, myself included, set out on the road to being a coach by being a 'trainer' first. Most of us were exposed to this type of instruction and guidance when we were young and as experiential learning we naturally follow suit. Tradition is the predominant driver for why we do what we do.

For me, a 'trainer' focuses only on the player, the game (or their version of the game) and the playing of the game, taking little or nothing else into account. They have a very narrow lens and unconsciously try to impose the game on the child. They often work from a set of drills and can run well organised, linear training sessions. They teach their players the parts of the game, and hope or believe that these parts will lead to better performance in the whole of the game. They, very much, lead their training sessions and see themselves as leaders of the group, there to impart their knowledge and tell the players what to do and what not to do. Unconsciously, they try to 'force' the game 'into' the child. Consciously or unconsciously they want the children to be passive and submissive to them. A good session is one where the children are obedient. They often mistake performance in a training session for learning, retention and development.

Think 'lectures and lines', rules and control. At some level they don't want the children ruining 'their training session'. They lecture while often saying nothing of great relevance or intelligence. They give 'the answers' but not the appropriate challenge or assistance. I like to say that sometimes they unconsciously act as if they've invented the game and their goal is to drill it into the children. In many ways they take themselves too seriously. Often, their intentions are good but they are misguided and their delivery is poor. Their self-awareness is low. They have no framework for improvement.

For me, the traditional 'trainer' looks at the world through a straw. They believe constant repetition of drills will lead to ultimate performance and are often left disappointed, frustrated or perhaps even deluded. You must understand, drills do not necessarily make you better at skills. They do not necessarily transfer into learning, retention and better performance in, and engagement with, the game long term. There are many more facets to it.

My point in all this is not to prove traditional 'training' won't lead to improvement, because often it will. My point is to raise awareness of the fact that if we change our perspective and broaden our scope, a much better way will become clear and change and improvement will follow.

The much better way I talk of is 'Coaching'. Coaching is simply looking through a much broader lens, or set of lenses, than the 'trainer' does. The quicker you come to this awareness the better. Understanding and appreciating the difference can be the making of a coaching career. It definitely was for me. You have to be aware something exists before you can truly embrace it.

When seeking to understand a concept, definitions are always useful. So too is simplicity. My own personal definition of coaching is simply,

"Raising awareness through challenging and assisting appropriately."

This may appear somewhat vague to you at present, but through reading the book, I hope it makes great sense and provides you with a new perspective. Coaching is guiding not controlling, it is inspiring not forcing. It is finding the sweet spot where you stretch them enough to nurture growth. Truly great coaches coach the game 'out of' the child, through intelligent practice design and providing the correct learning environment; by providing the appropriate challenge and assistance over time. They are 'environment creators'. They understand the aim of coaching is to develop self-reliance and autonomy, not dependence.

Coaching is a craft and the aim of this book is to assist you in developing your craft. There are numerous elements. In order to continue to improve, you must be willing to learn and grow. Coaching a child should be an enjoyable and satisfying experience for the coach. It is developmental in nature and not overtly performance driven. You must learn to appreciate and understand the difference. The better you get, the better it gets. Unfortunately, many would-be coaches never get to this place. It is my contention that many are unaware this place even exists. I hope that this book will at the very least raise your awareness.

My primary goal throughout the book will be to make you think! I am coaching you to coach; to find your own solutions, to be a problem solver, an 'awareness raiser' (we will see this later). To be someone who can give assistance without causing resentment. To practice a 'transformational leadership style' where the children are assisted and challenged in a warm manner to be the best they can be. I am coaching you to look at it as more a relationship than rules based practice.

I will conclude with a simple exercise. The book is full of simple exercises that will help you create your 'coaching world'. They are designed to draw your attention to what you feel is important. This is integral I can't give you the answers. It is akin to me giving you direction to a location from my house when you are leaving from your own house. It will not work.

You must create your own 'coaching world'. I urge you to get a pencil (your answers may change over time) and take the time to complete the exercises as you read through the book. This book is a tool to be used not admired. I understand the human condition wants you to skip the exercises, and continue on reading apace to 'find the answers'. Perhaps this may happen on first reading and that is ok. However, I am confident if you take the time to answer the questions, you will surprise yourself with the level of your answers. You see, we know most of this already it is just that we don't practice it or we don't have a method for practicing it. In coaching, everything we do is learning, problem solving and practice. There are no right or wrong answers for these exercises and indeed your answers will change over time as you grow and evolve as a coach.

1. Describe the characteristics of a great child coach.

Experienced, compassionate, objective, curious

2. How does a great child coach talk and act towards his/her players?

Supportive, curious, listening, guiding

3. How does a great child coach make their players feel?

Heard, hopeful, excited, engaged, belonging, hungry

4. How does a great child coach act in stressful and challenging situations?

Calm, objective, clarity, quick

5. How does a great child coach motivate his/ her players?

By player

6. Describe how a great child coach would make important team-related decisions.

To conclude this short introductory chapter, I ask you to take a minute to assess what you believe to be the difference between a trainer and a coach. Keep adding to this list as you read through the book the differences can often be subtle, but over time the results from both are extremely different. Time magnifies everything, good and bad.

Trainer	Coach
	Growth
	Leadership
	Engagement
	Curiosity
	Learning
	Vision
	Patience
	Investment

Anyone can go out and buy a book of drills and be a trainer. Coaching is much more. As I hope to show throughout the book, coaching can change the lives of children and players for the better. It can also change the life of the coach for the better too once you get on the pathway of learning and improvement.

"The trainer leads by direction, the coach by inspiration -Rules v Relationships"

The difference is key!

Can you see?

CHAPTER 2
THE CARVER FRAMEWORK

Now that we have somewhat established what coaching is, and indeed isn't, we can explore what I believe are the qualities of a top coach or, more to the point, what it is they do consistently well.

An open or 'Growth Mindset' is a must for learning (for coach and player) so if you wish to reach your potential in coaching children you must first develop a 'can do attitude'. The 'How can I?' questions must be continuously flying around in your head. You must be willing to set high standards for yourself.

Let me now warn you that learning and changing are challenging pursuits which require engagement, resilience and drive. Change isn't easy and good coaches can't be lazy. There is no progress without change. Transition is a slow process; for player and coach. However, the only alternative is not learning. In coaching children, I believe we have a moral obligation to improve and get better.

In my search to simplify, refine and get to the core of coaching and coaching practices I have come up with my own acronym for coaching, the word CARVER -Connection, Awareness, Research, Values and Visions, Endorsing, Reflection.

I call it The CARVER Framework of Coaching. These six areas cover what I believe encapsulates the essence of good coaching and provides a platform for learning and improvement in coaching. Some of the areas overlap and intertwine, looking at the same subject from different angles, but I feel they are distinct in their own right and merit study, consideration and discussion.

The CARVER Framework aims to be a set of highly usable lenses and tools for the coach. It can enable the coach to; see the things they need to be able to see, how they need to be able to see them, and then intervene accordingly. One thing I have learned in coaching is that we don't see things as they are; we see things as we are. Great coaches are excellent observers or 'noticers'. It is a skill you must develop.

The analogy of the coach I use is comparing them to the wood or stone Carver. The coach works with the child to realise potential. They help 'pull the player out' of the child. They have the vision to see potential; to see things for what they could be and the ability to help realise this.

VISION

> *"I saw the angel in the marble and carved until I set him free."*
> **Michelangelo- Italian Sculptor, Painter and Architect (on his sculpture of David)**

The Carver doesn't force (or perhaps only when required). They make endless little improvements and adjustments. They shape. They have a vision of what they want to create and they work consistently, purposefully, skilfully and patiently. There is little instant gratification. They help realise potential. They have short-term focus while all the time having a long-term vision or a 'future focus'. The Carver pulls the masterpiece out of the raw material. The Carver is a craftsman. Coaching is a craft and like all crafts it must be developed over time. You must serve your apprenticeship. You can develop into a craftsman.

"Coaching is a craft. You must develop your craft."

9

Also and quite appropriately the Latin word for education is 'educere' which translates into 'draw out' or 'lead out'. For me the analogy is totally congruent. Carving, teaching and coaching are simply about realising potential.

The CARVER Framework is a set of lenses, and framework through which to view, inform, plan and assess your coaching. It is your coaching perspective and framework for improvement. Again perspective is hugely important. If you change the way you look at things, the things you look at will change.

The CARVER Coaching Framework allows you to see and assess:

- Are you connecting, and seeing and forming connections?
- Are you self- aware and role-aware?
- Are you raising awareness in your players?
- Where are you with your research? Are you following best practice and best principles? Are your coaching sessions providing the appropriate challenges?
- Are you being true to your personal values and visions? Have you a 'future focus'?
- Have you a clear vision for your session?
- Are you endorsing what you want? Are you precise in affirming positive actions?
- Are you reflecting? Are you using personal feedback to feed forward and ensure that you are actively and continuously learning and improving?

Often the answer will be no. You are not perfect, this book isn't perfect, but by following its key messages you will be continually and consciously trying to improve your 'coaching world'. You will not be strong in all areas but you can improve in all areas. Coaching is all about continuous improvement and not perfection. There are no magic formulas. You must be willing to work at your craft.

Coaches must be humble. It is never about you. You are there to serve and put others first. The CARVER Framework has the capacity to allow you to be humble and dissipate the ego. It can also allow you to coach the game you love with love. Love is essential. It allows the children you coach; play the game they love with love. I believe this.

What follows is the CARVER Framework in child coaching in sport explained as simply as I can, yet in as much detail as I believe necessary. I hope it is a useful tool for you and trust it will be. I hope it can give you new eyes or a new view point and a practical framework for continued improvement.

Can you see what I see?

Perspective is key

Can you see?

CHAPTER 3
CONNECTION

Your ability to connect and to see and create connections will be a huge determent of your success in coaching. Coaches must create connections in everything they do. Connections create culture.

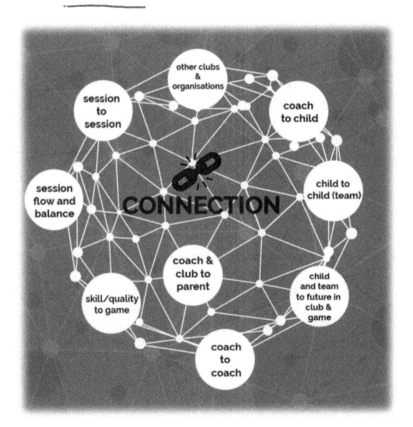

Coach to Child Connection

Coaching is a relationship between two people, in our case, the coach and the child. Even in a large group setting coaching is still a relationship between two people. If you are coaching thirty children, you are coach to every one of them individually. You are 'their coach' as well as the team coach. When you appreciate and understand this you come to see that the relationship game is the first game you must win as coach. You are looking to build the child at every level. You must connect. This connection will precede true engagement, commitment and contribution. You can't afford to miss this one. It drives confidence in the child and in the coach as well. We feel at ease.

"Connection drives confidence. Confidence drives competence (and vice versa)."

Connection takes time and awareness. Often I do one-off coaching sessions with youth teams, and I struggle to connect because I don't know them and they don't know me. My coaching style is stifled due to lack of connection. I need to be, or come across as, more authoritarian than I would like. When I know children and am connected to them my style is free and fluid and they understand me.

How do we connect? For me, when dealing with children it's through fun, kindness and love. Kindness comes in many forms and everyone has it at some level and in some style. Find it in you and practise it. Everyone understands kindness. It is a language that speaks to all.

How can you show kindness to children/ players?

_____

_____

Fun comes more naturally to some than others, but we all have a fun side. Use your personality here. Let yourself go. It's not about being politically correct; it's about being human. You will have different type relationships with different children. Some children will be more receptive to different types of interpersonal interactions. Some will be serious; some will be more playful. Some will be shy and retiring others will be more gregarious and naturally engaging. A rule of thumb is; if the child is mature or developed enough to receive the interaction then the interaction is appropriate. Please don't try to be perfect or try to be what you think people expect. Be free and be yourself but be aware none the less. Child sport is meant to be fun. In fact, all sport, and indeed life, is meant to be fun. Fun is fundamental. Never lose sight of this. Play fun, socialising games with the children (*see appendix*). Get to know the child and allow them to get to know you. Child Coaching is all about the individual. You are not coaching a player; you are coaching a child.

"Connect with the child, develop the child; improve the player. Be kind!"

Love is also an important concept in connection. It is love in the sense of the ancient Greek term 'Agape' which is unconditional love that transcends and persists regardless of circumstance. Coaches love the game and therefore must love their players. Coaching with love will create connection. This connection you develop with the child will allow you to challenge and stretch them when needs be and they will understand you are coming from a good place with feedback that might otherwise be met with resentment.

Put simply; coach the game you love with love. For me coaching with love means striving to have nothing but positive intentions for the players you coach and owning their challenges as your own. Coaching the game, you love, with love, allows the children to play the game, they love, with love. We must help nurture this love of the game in them. This love will breed persistence which is a prerequisite for reaching their potential. This love will breed learning. Coaching from a point of love will give you peace of mind and solace. You literally cannot lose. You are a developmental coach and simply want what is best for the child.

You should come up with some sort of method or system to connect with every child you coach at every session. In my role as teacher, I developed a system to do this. I always ask that every child says hello to me every morning on entering the classroom, and goodbye and thanks every evening. I also ask them come up to me at my desk with their homework every morning. It is my chance to look them in the eye and connect with them straight away. It guarantees connection before the day's work even begins we are now in a position to work together.

Adapting this concept into your coaching you can insist that every child says hello to you on entering the field daily. A quick hello, some eye contact and a quick 'High Five' (a fist touch / handshake). The coach/child connection is made automatically and can now develop throughout the session. Over time, even the shy and introverted child will look you in the eye and say a few words. The more extroverted will say much more! With structure and practice each connection will grow stronger and stronger over time.

Without such a system you may find yourself half way through a session not even knowing if certain players are there, and may never even acknowledge the child throughout the session. Can you see the need for systematic connection?

"Connect with the children. No Connection=No Coaching."

Another simple means of developing connection pre training is to actively float around the players for the five or ten minutes before training starts having a little word with them, a laugh or a joke or helping them with something they are struggling with. This practice will see your connection with the players develop.

Do you currently, actively and consciously, connect with each child at your session? If not, come up with a way you can systematically connect with each player at each session?

"How are you doing?"

As previously stated, in order to connect, you must get to know the child. To this end information on them is key; their likes, their dislikes and so on. The simplest way to do this is to have them fill out a Player Profile Sheet. This sheet must obviously be age appropriate and for the very young their parents can help them with it. You can choose to keep them private or share them with the rest of the team. There is so much you can do with this profiling concept if you are willing to put in a little effort (or indeed get someone to help you- always seek help). You can build private personal profiles for each player from your own observations which will be useful in helping you understand them and thereby connect better and coach them better.

Opposite is a sample Player Profile for a 10-year-old. For the younger children you can make it simpler for the older ones make it more advanced if you please. Draft your own one; ask the questions you want answers for. Illicit the information that will help you connect with the child.

PLAYER PROFILE
Name-
Date of Birth-
Family Members-
School you attend-
Why you play (given sport)-
Do you play other sports?
Favourite Player-
Favourite Food-
Favourite Song-
Favourite Film-
I am good at ......
What I find hard.........
What's the one thing my coach should know about me to help them coach me better.

Child to Child Connection- Connecting the Team

On deeper consideration of the 'Lens of Connection' we come to appreciate that in team sport we are trying to connect the individuals as a tightly knit unit; as a team. In broad terms a team can be defined as having; a number of people with complementary skills who are committed to a common purpose, performance goals, and a common approach for which they hold themselves mutually accountable. A coach creates and constructs a team through creating connections.

Surely we want our children to be friends therefore a coach must strategically facilitate socialisation between the players. Showing up to a training session, going straight into action and never facilitating interpersonal connection is a mistake. Can you see this? You must appreciate that once a child is comfortable in their surroundings and knows they belong everything will be fine. We are all the same really, we all want to belong. This is not to say they won't reach some level of connection through simply playing the game and training together, they will. However, it may primarily be a sport based connection and you may find the better players will gravitate to each other and the weaker players will be isolated.

Creating cohesion and equality within the group contributes to much of its success. Purposeful and proactive socialisation of the group will actively help eradicate cliques and gangs that will cause some children to become isolated. It will actively assist in eradicating bullying, social isolation and other unpleasant issues. Will you still encounter bullying type behaviour? Yes, you may, is the answer, because it is a fact of life. However, appropriate social skills can be learned and relatively improved and so must be coached daily in our sessions. A great coach coaches more than the game and the player.

Purposefully facilitating, nurturing and supporting social interaction between the children will allow them to connect at a higher level. Team connectedness creates individual and collective confidence. Play and games are an excellent way to achieve this with children. Physical Literacy or Fundamental Movement Skill games *(see appendix)* which facilitate socialisation and fun are vital here. Under your guidance, these games bring fun and laughter and build connection. Coaches can, and should, join in to. The children love this. You will see the 'fun, kindness and love' grow between player and coach, and player and player. The connection will grow.

Do you consciously socialise the group at each session?
Jot down some ideas to help you socialise the group and create team connectedness.

_____

_____

Coaching is so much more than just about the given sport. We are creating a bond, or more accurately, a number of bonds. We are connecting everything. We are creating a culture of friendship. We are creating unity. My absolute favourite saying with regard to team sport is,

"In Unity there is Strength."

The coach must show he values every child by mentioning them by name frequently and endorsing their positive actions. This gives the child an identity within the group. Regardless of their ability, they are treated with the same respect. We value them and the children learn to value each other because we are raising that awareness among them. The children will grow to value what the coach values.

The Team Charter Creating the Brand, The Bond and The Unity
The absolute best way to facilitate connection within the Team is to allow children to create their own charter or 'Team Brand'. It shows the children that you value their opinion and that you trust them.

A facilitated meeting and discussion focused on between five to ten pertinent questions will do the trick. Involve them in the process as opposed to imposing beliefs or rules upon them. This gives them autonomy and affords you a firm grounding for holding players accountable to team standards.

Make it into a small group work exercise. Allow them build their own world. Over time they will learn to live very happily in it, once you are committed to holding them accountable to it.

Examples of Questions that may be used for creating a team charter are:

1. List three ways a great teammate contributes or gives to their team. (Being a good teammate is all about giving, sometimes you must explain this to the children. Consciously raise their awareness of the concept of 'giving' and your team and players will 'get' a lot. Help them understand. I call it the 'give to get scale'. If they understand this, they understand much about sport and life).
2. What is unacceptable, acceptable and exceptional behaviour for a teammate in training/ game etc.?
3. What type of atmosphere do you want to train and play in?

4. What do we want to do well as a team/what do we want the team to stand for/ what standards do we want to live by and why are these things important?
5. What does success mean for our team/ what does it look like for us? What is winning for us?
6. What would you like management to say about you at the end of the year?
7. What is unacceptable behaviour for team management? (I'll throw this one in here although it doesn't relate to team brand. It is always a question which the answer intrigues me.)

Do you currently give the children input into their team brand? Write the questions you might ask your team to begin to build a team identity.

_____

_____

We are raising awareness (we will see this next) among the players about all the elements of a good team. We are building a team culture organically. We are engineering the environment in an intelligent manner. We are giving them ownership of, and connectedness to the team and developing leadership qualities.

These culture building exercises can be simple or as complex as you wish. You don't need to be an expert to facilitate them but it does require diligence on your part. You can ask the above questions or come up with better ones yourself. All children should get a print out of the charter. It is important this document is treated with respect.

If you wish you can design an exercise to target specific areas. For example, you can pick the area of 'being a good teammate' and get input through group work on the various qualities and characteristics of a good teammate. List the qualities given and each session you could highlight one and have a reward for the player that exhibited that quality the most in the session. Endorse their positive actions.

End of year awards can be specifically connected back to team brand values making them meaningful, learning based and achievable by all. Children love to be rewarded and acknowledged for their positive actions. It is hugely motivating for them.

Perhaps you could enlist the help of some parents with the appropriate skill set who might love to give input in this type of project. Gather good people around you and your coaching and utilise their skill- set. When we look at 'Reflection' we will see how we can ensure we are following through on the aspirations of our team brand.

Non-Sporting Social Outing
You can and should plan social outings and gatherings for the team that are apart and away from the sport. Taking the sport out of it makes them very much 'children' as opposed to 'players'. This is important, as it allows them to get to get to know each other at a deeper level. It breaks many boundaries. What are the advantages of a non-sporting social outing for your team?

_____

_____

Where would be good to bring the team on a social outing?

_____

_____

Jot some other team culture building exercise ideas here.

_____

_____

Connect the Child and the Team
to their Future in the Sport and Club

Show the child their future in the sport and the club. Paint a picture for them. It is truly motivating and inspiring for them. They must be motivated to continue to strive and work towards bigger and better things. That hunger must be nurtured in them. Talk about ten years' time, when they will (may) be playing senior for the club and playing to the best of their ability. Help them grow their love for the club. Make them feel like they belong, like they are connected and at home and inspire them to want to contribute. Align them with the adult section of the club. You want to create that idenfication with place; that connection to.... Tell them you'll be there in the stand watching and smiling and high fiving all the other coaches who have coached them through the years. Show them their club wants and needs them. Make them see and appreciate it. Show them the history of the club and make them aware that they are part of something bigger than themselves and of the positives they can gain by contributing to the club. Help them connect to it. Many of them will grow to love it.

With this said, it must be noted that we can't consciously hold a child hostage to the game or the club or manipulate them in any way. They have free will and are fully entitled to do as they please so there is a fine balance here. You are really showing them they have a future here if they decide to pursue it.

Do you currently connect the children to their future in the game and club? If not, what is the value in doing this?

_____

_____

Do you currently connect the children to the history, culture and adult section of the club? Do you show them they are part of something bigger than themselves? If not what might be the value in doing this?

_____

_____

Connecting with your Fellow Coaches as a Coaching Team

Chances are you will be coaching your team with the assistance of a number of other coaches or helpers. If not, your first job is to recruit help. Enlist people with different skills sets that can add value and may enjoy tasks that perhaps you don't have the time, inclination or skill set for.

Connection in a coaching team is vital. If you are 'Head Coach' it is your responsibility to plan the coaching session and incorporate your fellow coaches. This plan can have clear roles and responsibilities for each coach. Coaches can be furnished with the plan and aligned to its broad objectives. In this way, all coaches feel connected to the team and the session, and can bring their own unique qualities to the table. This is a practice you must invest a little time and thought into it while working towards making it simple and maintainable. We will look at session planning later and also look at the Coaching Team Model, which is where you really want to be heading to with this, 'Cohesive Collective Coaching'.

Do you currently actively and purposefully connect your coaching team? What can you see as the advantages of providing a structure whereby your fellow coaches can add value and utilise their skill set for the betterment of the team?

_____

_____

Connecting with Parents

"Win the child, win the parent" is a good motto but it is also true to say, "win the parent, win the child". Your connection with the parent is very important. You don't need to be great friends with them but if you present yourself as a competent person who has the best interests of the child at heart then you are on a winner. Something as simple as a beginning of year meeting where you outline your programme for the year can create the bond. If you prepare properly for it I am confident it will be a most useful exercise. When people understand, they support.

Create a simple Parent Booklet sharing with them your values and visions, your expectations and how you do things. This will help them understand, appreciate and support. You are raising awareness among the parents and awareness will lead to greater connection. They can become your greatest allies.

Lack of information causes misunderstanding, confusion and disconnect. It is your interest as coach to ensure parental connection. As already acknowledged, you can't do everything, so perhaps enlist the help of a parent with the appropriate skill set and interest to help you with this.

What are the benefits of aligning parents to your coaching practices?

_____

_____

Connecting Everything to The Game

Everything we do in a training session must be rooted in, and connected to performance in the game. You must be able to justify every detail of the session and then you must contextualise things for children, especially as they mature. You must show them how it relates to the game, where it fits in or where it transfers into the ame. In order to be fully motivated, players need to be aware of the connection to the real game situation. They must believe in what they are doing and why they are doing it. Raise their awareness. In teaching we use the term WALT, which stands for 'we are learning to'. In doing this, we are explaining to them what we are trying to achieve and why. Your research (see research chapter) will help you see these connections very clearly and allow you share them with the children.

Your 'connection lens' will become clearer and clearer the more you use it, and you will soon be able to make beautiful connections to performance. For example, you will see how a nice piece of footwork or an act of courage in a tag game will transfer to performance. You will see the leadership qualities emerge when you give a child the responsibility of lining out their team for an in-session game. This will drive your ability to 'endorse' sky high, which in turn, will allow your children to flourish.

Better still, you can ask them can they see where it fits in. Over time they will become very aware of how the different elements transfer into performance. Their awareness of connections will lead them to embrace, appreciate and engage with the game at a higher level. It will drive their precision and application to whatever skill execution they are doing. This is vitally important for motivation and learning. They will learn when there is a reason why. Contextualising is just so important.

We will see shortly the value of the Constraints Led Approach to coaching; a method that espouses representative practice design where training is designed to be as game like as possible. Again, learning is to be in context and contextualised for the children.

Are you aware of power of contextualising and connecting elements to the game? What is to be gained by the coach connecting sporting and non-sporting skills and qualities back to the game?

_____

_____

Connecting the Elements of Training within the Session Plan

Each coaching session must have balance between physical, social, technical/skill, tactical/team play and mental, at a very minimum. The effectiveness of the session depends on the connection of all the elements and the balance between them. This is not to say you can't tilt a session in a given direction, but all the elements need to be there and they need to be connected. A coach must be able to build and connect the session through precise planning. The session must flow. Your research and planning will help you here (we will look at these shortly).

Connecting Coaching Sessions to Each Other

This connection is the top end and one we are all looking to master; connecting session to session and ultimately all of our sessions into a comprehensive and appropriate training programme. This becomes increasingly important as we aim to stretch the older children.

Through your coaching you are obviously looking for improvement, retention and transfer into performance. The truth of the matter is we don't really know how effective our current training session has been until the following session. Has what we were aiming to coach been retained to a satisfactory level? In order to assess this, after the warm up, you can put in a challenge or conditioned game, without discussion or prompting, which allows them the opportunity to work on the skills or scenario you worked on in the previous session. Your job now is to observe how good recall and retention has been from the previous session and then you can work from this point and put in interventions based on what we see.

I really like this concept and methodology because over time the children learn that training and practice is all about learning and improvement as opposed to simply doing. It helps to develop intelligent, engaged players. They get a deeper appreciation of improvement and an awareness of their absolute central role in it. Over time this heightens their attentional focus and application to the session.

At a basic level you can ask:

- What am I going to do today and why?
- How does it relate to what I did in the previous session?
- How will I know if they have retained any of what I was attempting to coach previously?
- How does it relate to what I'm going to do next week and beyond?

It really comes down to researching, refining and reflecting; through knowing what you trying to achieve and how best to do this. Throughout the book we will tease out this topic, and although we may not fully give you the answer, I'm confident we can bring you to a greater level of awareness of it.

Connecting with Other Clubs, Sports and Organisations

Traditionally we look at other sports and organisations as our competitors, and while often not directly working against them, we certainly rarely actively work with them. In invasion sports we should certainly look to be connecting and partnering with local athletic, gymnastic, martial arts clubs, and so on. There is so much physical and athletic development to be gained by young players being involved in these types of activities and we can actively reach out and gain from building a strong connection with them. For example, all your players could do athletics for the winter months or off season, and they would be returning to you stronger and more physically literate than when they left. You can help facilitate this.

Multi-sport activity is also to be both promoted and facilitated among young players. It is widely recognised as best practice, so rather than see other sports as the opposition, we should be looking to work with them for the betterment of our players. Move away from fear of losing players to other codes. Instead, focus on improving what you as coach are offering to your players. Set high standards for yourself. If your product is good enough, your customer will buy it. We will see more on Physical Literacy and Multi Sport Activity in our chapter on research and hopefully you will appreciate how connecting with other clubs, organisations is a potential advantage.

Do you currently work with or against other clubs, sports and organisations in your community? List the advantages of connecting with these organisations.

_____

_____

Making Connections as a Lens

Making connections is a powerful concept. Connections are everywhere and they help us understand at a deeper level. Use your lens.

Summary Points

1. Coaching is an interpersonal relationship. Connect with every player.
2. Facilitate socialisation: Connect the team. Try a team charter.

3. We would like them to play the game long term. Connect them to their future in the game, the team and the club.
4. Connect with your fellow coaches and utilise their skillsets. Together we can achieve so much.
5. Connect with the parents. Make them your ally.
6. Connect everything you do in training back to the game or sport. The children must understand why they are doing it.
7. Connect the session. Balance the mental, physical, technical/ skills, and tactical/team play. The session must flow.
8. Connect your training sessions into a comprehensive, progressive and logical program.
9. Connect with other sports, clubs and organisations. Stop looking at them with fear.

Connection is key!

Can you see?

CHAPTER 4
AWARENESS

For me the concept of awareness encapsulates coaching pretty succinctly. Understanding this concept will bring you to the next level as a coach and bring the children to the next level as players and people. Building self-awareness into your coaching and players is a precursor to excellence. Your awareness lens will set you apart as a coach. It is the essence of coaching.

Have you ever ended up in a place you didn't know existed? Chances are you were lost, or on your way to another place, when you arrived there. You stumbled across it. I genuinely believe it is a major challenge for the average volunteer to stumble across any significant level of excellence in coaching. I just feel there is so much involved for someone who is not a professional to assimilate by themselves.

There's just so much to see in coaching, so much to connect, so much to simplify, so much you may be unaware of, so much you didn't even know you didn't know. If you are unaware you are walking in the darkness, how you will ever seek the light?

I believe having a mentor is a huge benefit for any volunteer coach. Having a 'learned other' is obviously going to be helpful if you want to be that 'learned other' to the child and team. A mentor can help you find your way; help show you there is a better way. However, the question is often "where do I find that mentor?" and, the answer is often, they don't exist in your proximity.

Nowadays, we see so many awareness campaigns: Cancer Awareness, Mental Health Awareness, Road Safety Awareness and so on. There is an awareness day or week for virtually everything and these bring information and truth into the collective conscious. Raising awareness leads to improvement and solutions. As human beings, we don't know what we don't know. How could we? I have heard of a Malayan saying something to the effect of;

'If you do not know what you do not know, then you won't know. If you do know what you do not know then you will know.'

This book is my attempt at a Coaching Awareness Campaign. Awareness is the greatest agent for change.

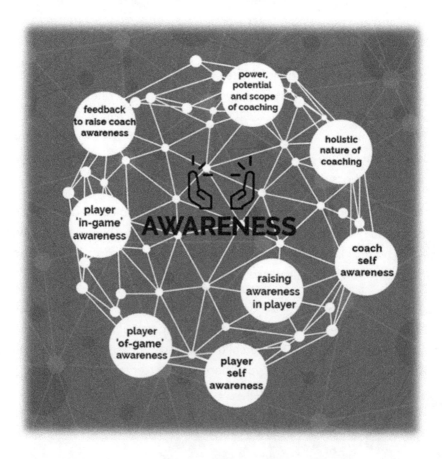

Awareness of the Power, Potential and Scope of Coaching

It is my absolute belief that as a society we have a total lack of appreciation and awareness of the power, potential and scope of child coaching in sport. How could we? So few of us have ever witnessed it performed truly well.

Now let us take a brief look at something you may not have considered deeply enough, if at all. I will share with you two simple, personal examples of the power, potential and scope of coaching children in sport. I genuinely don't share these with you to impress you at any level, I share them with you because they were two moments in my career that made me sit back and think "Wow, how powerful is this?" and inspired me to look at my coaching at a deeper level. In coaching you can do so much good; or harm. 'One Good Adult' can have such a powerful influence.

Below is a result from a four-week Physical Literacy (Exercise) Programme (a one-hour session per week over the course of four weeks, four sessions in total) I ran with a Child Agency that works with children with coordination and movement difficulties. The programme was overseen by occupational therapists, who performed pre and post testing on the children. I coached the children through an exercise programme I designed. Yes, they tested and re- tested what are perhaps more quantifiable things like throwing, catching, jumping and so on. And they showed positive improvement but for me this chart simplifies the power, scope and potential of coaching beautifully.

Question to children- On a scale of 1 to 10, with 1 not being confident at all and 10 being very confident how would you rate your ability to play sports?

	Week One Pre Programme	Week Four Post Programme
Child A	6	10
Child B	7	10
Child C	4	10
Child D	6	10
Child E	1	7

When these results came through, I was so happy. It highlighted to me the power, potential and scope of child coaching. Confidence leads to competence and vice versa. Confidence drives engagement and action. This feedback drove my self-awareness, which in turn drove my coaching to a new level. In four sessions the collective subjective confidence of five children to play sport had gone from twenty-four out of fifty, to forty-seven out of fifty. The group's confidence had doubled. There was a subjective 47% improvement in perceived confidence after four hours of coaching. I was genuinely amazed. For me this was a crystal clear example of the unlimited power of coaching. I had simply given them the appropriate challenges and assistance and their competence had led to confidence. I had also obviously connected with them at some level and I had created an environment that had 'pulled out' their confidence.

Next, I will share with you extracts from a letter left on my table, on the last day of school, by a twelve-year-old girl who had been involved in a school project I ran with the goal of making our school healthier and happier. I never formally taught her in class, and for most of the two years she was involved in the project we met only once a week for about fifteen minutes. I was Head Coach and they were my Junior Coaches, and the project involved things like coaching children exercise at break, leading activity breaks in classrooms, and promoting healthy eating. In my role I'd simply allocate the jobs to the Junior Coaches, ensure they knew their role and say "well done!" and "thanks" when they were finished. I actually gave them minimal instruction. I gave them ownership of the project. I afforded them the opportunity to be experiential learners. I merely provided the environment. I simply and consistently challenged them to do their best and assured them that this would be good enough. I would help or assist them only as needed. We would systematically reflect on our doing and ask ourselves how can we do it better? Simple really!

Here are a few words of what she wrote,

"I just thought that you of all people I will really miss because if it wasn't for you, I would still be the shy girl ... Before I knew nothing about exercise or how to talk to a group...I had no confidence in myself...But look at me now... I wanted to quit so many times because I was so bad but every time something that you said always made me change my mind and for that I thank you."

This is powerful stuff for a twelve-year-old to write in a letter and leave on an adult's table without a word. Again this feedback drove my awareness of the power, potential and scope of child coaching, and in turn drove my coaching to a new level.

Awareness of the Holistic Nature of Coaching

Child coaching in sport can, should and must develop the physical, tactical, technical/ skill, but also the social and the emotional. It must be a holistic practice and must start and finish with the child. Common wisdom tells us it is good for children to be part of a team sport, but I feel we have no idea how powerful it can be and rarely appreciate its true scope.

It is beyond question that the coach can have a powerful positive effect on all areas of the child's life; the power of 'One Good Adult' It goes without saying that if we are doing virtually any type of exercise with them, it will have a positive physical effect in the short term. But we can do so much more. We can develop the children so they go on to become self-aware, confident, and happy children/adults/players. We can give them every chance at success in sport and in life. We can play our part in enhancing society.

The non-physical qualities we can develop through a child centred holistic approach to coaching far exceed the physical and technical qualities. Coached properly, the child who is turning into the teen will reach the 'end of the beginning' of their involvement in sport as opposed to the 'beginning of the end'. According to a poll from the National Alliance for Youth Sports in America, around 70% of children in the United States stop playing organised sports by the age of thirteen.

Below are but a few areas and qualities we can develop through a holistic, child centred approach to coaching the child. Without doubt, there are many more. The more we look the more we can see. Our awareness is heightened as our perspective changes. If we create the proper environment, all these qualities can be developed. We can coach life lessons through sport or perhaps more accurately we must learn to coach life lessons through sport. As coaches, we can help children learn about themselves through sport so they can be better, balanced and more successful people in society later. We are coaching self-awareness. The absolute best part about this is that if we develop these areas, the child will go on to be a much better player long term. We will see this more when move onto our Visions section.

- Respect and Fairness- Coach them to respect people and things. Coach them to take care of their gear and equipment and to clean up after themselves. Coach them to respect the opposition and embrace them as their teacher. Give them a healthy perspective on competition and endeavour and they will grow to love it.

- Appreciation- Coach them the value of saying "thanks". If they say thanks it shows that they have value on what they are receiving. If they value something they get good from it. Saying thanks simply acknowledges all the good things they are receiving. If they constantly acknowledge all the good things in their life the odds are, they will have a good life.

- Interpersonal and Communication Skills- Our interpersonal relations with others are probably the greatest source of happiness we can hope to have in life. Facilitate the development of interpersonal and communication skills through providing the need for it in your coaching sessions; the dialogical environment. Design pair and group work games and tasks in training. Let them coach each other. By providing a need to communicate through your coaching methodology you are, by degrees, coaching it. Will they struggle with it at first? Yes; they are learners. Everything we learn to do we learn by doing badly. Be patient!

- Teamwork and Leadership Skills- It is hugely important to allow children to lead and be leaders. It shows them the challenges of leadership, and therefore, they learn to appreciate those who lead. Everything in sport and life rises and falls on leadership. Set challenges for them to figure out and then be patient. Perhaps give them prior notice of the challenge you are going to set them before the session and give them a little advice and help; the appropriate assistance. Set them up for success and watch them learn.

Teamwork is required in every walk of life, so develop it through providing the need for it in your coaching. Teamwork is often talked about but rarely coached. For teamwork to occur, the conditions and the environment must be right. Create the need for teamwork by using games that require it _(see appendix)._ Opportunity is the mother of all improvement.

- Self-esteem and Confidence- Confidence breeds competence and drives action. Everything follows confidence. If you challenge and assist appropriately they will grow in confidence.
- Self-Discipline and Self Control- Having the drive to do the 'need to do's' as well as the 'nice to do's'. Being able to discipline yourself so that others won't have to.
- Personal Responsibility and Self Reliance- Coach the child that they and they alone are responsible for themselves. *"No one can do it for you" "If it is to be it is up to me".*
- Mental and Physical Resilience, Robustness, and Resolve- When coaching kids, we need to actively, consciously and routinely coach and build physical and mental resilience. Children will cry and lie down easily if they get hit (obviously I am not talking about when a child is genuinely hurt or injured here) or perceive they have been fouled or wronged. I am not being insensitive here; we are coaching them to learn to cope with the demands of the game and purposely building a culture and environment of resilience, robustness and toughness. Warm up exercises can and should include "get back up" type exercises. Simple stuff... on your belly/ back/ back knees etc.- get back up. Drill the importance of 'getting back up' (to the feet) into them in a fun manner. From the beginning they learn to pride themselves on always getting back up and going again. Coach the understanding that when they are on the ground they are out of the game. Raise their awareness that they are playing a contact game. "It's a contact game" is a phrase I purposefully use when coaching children. Every time a child falls or gets hit encourage them to get straight up and endorse those who do ('Shine a light on what is right'). We are coaching life skills. Resilience is critical in sport and life. Within a short period, they grow to understand and become aware that good players have courage, grit and resolve and keep going. The need for the

'magic water bottle' is lessened greatly and the children spend more time learning the game as opposed to sobbing and crying.

- Dealing with Winning and Losing, Success and Failure- Create scenarios where they are going to fail and then guide them through the process. You must coach them how to win and lose. In order to remain motivated, committed, engaged and focused we all have to learn to respond well to setbacks, including failing to achieve our goals. Having a clear 'vision for winning' is critical here (we will see this later).
- Mental Health and Wellbeing- A positive by-product from the sum of the above.

Great coaches are aware of the true power, potential and scope of child coaching in sport and fully believe in it. They are aware of its holistic nature and 'draw out' numerous non sporting qualities in their players.

List your top five most important non sporting qualities of a player?

_____

_____

Coach Self- Awareness

Now we have hopefully raised awareness of the power, potential and scope of coaching we need to raise awareness of the self. The key to coaching is self-awareness. Personal mastery is a hallmark of effective practitioners across all disciplines and is rooted in the discipline of continuous learning and improvement.

> *"It's not the mountain we conquer it's ourselves."*
> **Edmund Hillary- The first man to climb Mount Everest**

How would you feel about watching a video of yourself coaching? It would be a hugely beneficial exercise. Try it! Perhaps it mightn't make for pleasant viewing. How many children would be engaged? Would you be cool, calm, at ease, succinct and in flow? The list of questions is endless.

A question I've asked many volunteer coaches is, "If there was a hidden camera on your session do you think you would squirm watching it?" Most answer yes. However, this is great because it is the beginning of self-awareness. It is brutal honesty. Coaching is about self-improvement not self-preservation. However, self-preservation, is (unfortunately in this case) one of the first laws of nature.

We must learn to get over ourselves. What type of a coach do you actually want to be? This will be determined by your visions and values, which we will look at in detail shortly. Why do you coach children? Finding the answers to these questions will help you build your 'coaching world'. Coaching is a constant struggle between, who we are and who we want to be.

Never underestimate the importance of your role as coach. However, I must warn you about the importance of controlling your ego. In order to do so you must have a firm awareness of your 'Why'.

Why do you coach children?

_____

_____

Why do you coach the way you do?

_____

_____

You must also be aware of:

- Your 'talk to listen ratio', I can pretty much guarantee you it is way out of whack and I trust I don't have to explain which one

I feel is too dominant. Now I am not expecting you to listen to absolute 'gobbledygook' at length but you must have patience when listening to children. You must also appreciate that through your coaching you should be teaching them the vocabulary and terminology they need to discuss game related matters accurately. It is my contention that they should be able to hold a relatively intelligent conversation about the game by nine years of age. Patience is necessary, they will grow into the conversations we have with them. If you are predominantly a talker can you see the value of improving your listening skills?

- The language you use and how you communicate; of your 'precision in language'. Almost everything you do and say will either have a positive or negative effect on the child. Consider what might a transcript of your coaching session look like?
- That as coach your fairness, your kindness, your competence, and your values are there for all to see. Your coaching is always on show.

How you treat the weakest in the group? Do you actively and consciously treat them all relatively equal?

_____

_____

- That virtually everything that happens under your watch is your responsibility. The team will be a product of the environment you have created. The team will therefore reflect the coach over time. Take ownership of this fact.

What type of team environment are you creating?

_____

_____

How does it feel to be coached by you?

_____

_____

How might the children you currently coach describe you?

_____

_____

The list is endless and throughout the book we will continue to address it. Self-awareness is key. Rather than allowing this to put pressure on yourself, use it as motivation and guidance. Use awareness to lead you on a path of continuous improvement.

Coach Role- Awareness

Our job as child coaches is not to force a given sport on a child. Our job is to open it up to them and provide them with the skills and qualities required to be successful in that sport and in life in general. It is very important for you to appreciate this. When they reach their teens they will decide whether long term involvement in the sport is for them or not. If it is, you have provided them with every opportunity to reach their potential. If not you have provided them with many of the physical and non-physical qualities required to be live healthy and happy lives.

Your role as coach isn't to brainwash or force. Ultimately, your role as child coach is to develop the child's capacity to access the game long term if he/she should wish to do so. The number one priority is to leave the child happy while having strategically worked towards the long term interest of the player and the club. Child coaching is and must be developmental in philosophy.

My definition of the role of coach crystallizes my perspective on what my role is and I believe this lens allows me do it extremely well. My job is not to externally impose the game on the child. My role is simple to raise awareness while providing appropriate challenges and assistance.

What is your role as child coach?

_____

_____

This leads us to us to the really important bit; Awareness to Raise Awareness!

Raising Awareness Among Players

In coaching we are merely giving the child new perspective, drawing their attention, raising their awareness. Our job is to awaken the player in the child and bring them to a place of self-actualization. Our job is to use our knowledge to draw the children's attention to what is important. Our job is to heighten their engagement with the game through inspiring them and designing appropriate sessions. Our job is to 'pull' or 'draw' the player out. Our aim should be to raise; 'in- game awareness', 'of- game awareness' and 'self- awareness' (in the child). Coaching is not simply about what you know. That's only a fraction of it. It's really about what you do with what you know.

I didn't invent the game. You didn't invent the game. The game isn't ours to impose on children. The game belongs to the players and they must make their own of it. I view it that we are coaching the game 'out' of them not 'into' them. Like the Carver we are helping to develop and realise something that's already there, already inside and it is our responsibility to help expose it. Once more, my definition of coaching is –

"Raising awareness through challenging and assisting appropriately"

awareness

challenge

assist

So, for me, I am always trying to raise a state of awareness in the child and so awaken the player. Review the section on 'Power, Potential and Scope of Coaching' and appreciate how we can drive self-awareness in the child through nurturing the non-sporting characteristics.

Raising 'In- Game' Awareness

From a playing of view, my aim is to work towards developing better player 'in-game awareness'. The best way to develop 'in- game awareness' is by designing (representative) practice sessions that provide opportunities for real learning; 'the appropriate challenge and assistance'.

Without getting too deep into theory or seeking to confuse you I will further my concept of raising 'in-game awareness' through reference to Ecological Dynamics which underpins the Constraints Led Approach or Games Based Approach to coaching as it is sometimes commonly referred to. (Please note; technically these approaches do differ, but are none the less harmonious, and so for the purpose of simplicity I will use the terms inter-changeably.) Please appreciate that this can appear complex and may take a couple of readings in order to grasp.

Ecological Dynamics

Ecological Psychology is a field of psychology where, perception is considered to be a functional act of picking up information from the environment, to use for the regulation of movement. Ecological psychology places great emphasis on the interaction between the organism (in our case the child) and the environment. Actions are not isolated but instead they are seen as being nested in a series of interactions.

Dynamical Systems Theory is an ecological psychology theory of motor learning or skill acquisition (how we acquire skill). It is an explanation for how certain behaviours emerge in humans (and other organisms). The major premise of Dynamical Systems Theory is that the body is a complex system composed of millions of interacting parts. It proposes that the intelligence that coordinates the body is not localised in any one particular part, but emerges from the complex interactions of all the different parts, which 'self-organise'. Thus, unlike a simple machine, complex systems exhibit behaviours that are controlled without a central controller. Changes in state are often said to be nonlinear, which means that small inputs to the system can produce large outputs, or vice versa and non-linearity is a key underpinning concept.

Ecological Dynamics combines these two perspectives to understand phenomena that emerge in the transactions between individuals and their environments and to offer an integrated framework that suggests sports expertise is based on the human behaviours at the level of performer- environment interactions. It informs and underpins Non Linear Pedagogy and the Constraints Led Approach to Coaching (see shortly).

In a sporting context the playing environment determines what opportunities for action are available to the player and these opportunities are referred to as 'affordances'. The learning for players is in finding these opportunities or invitations for action or becoming what is termed 'attuned' to them. The key to learning is to become 'attuned to the affordances'. Again, 'affordances' are merely opportunities for action in the environment/ game. Affordances may be similar but they are never the same and are ever- present but will not be acted upon if the player is unaware of their existence.

The coach's role is to help the learner perceive or become aware of the affordances, not by telling them but by guiding them towards perceiving the affordances for themselves. To the ecological dynamical theorists, practice is all about learning and this learning is of the implicit kind. Put in the language of normal people implicit learning is...'getting good at something without being told how' or 'learning by doing'.

At this point the work and teachings of the Soviet neurophysiologist Nikolai Bernstein must be acknowledged. Bernstein was one of the pioneers in the field of motor learning (acquiring skills) and his work has guided many of those who have come after him. He theorized that in order to become more skilled training does not consist of repeating a solution to a motor problem ad nauseam but in the process of solving this problem again and again or in repeating a problem that needs to be solved differently. In the context of motor control 'during a correctly organised exercise, a student is repeating many times, not the means for solving a given motor problem, but the process of its solution, the changing and improvement of the means' (Bernstein). Therefore, practice of any movement or skill should basically be what he termed 'repetition without repetition' and not simply a rehearsal of a movement pattern. In other words, we learn not by repeating patterns of movement, but by repeating the process of solving the motor problem. Skill develops through repetition of the process of solving movement problems and so if you accept Bernstein's idea that motor

↳ cadence !

45

learning is not about memorising a solution but rather learning how to solve problems then your job as a coach in designing practice is to create challenging problems for your players.

The Constraints Led Approach (CLA)

The Constraints Led Approach (CLA) to coaching is a contemporary pedagogical approach underpinned by Non-Linear Pedagogy and Ecological Dynamics. Non- linear Pedagogy is non-repetitive practice with a high level of contextual interference where the players will have spells of improving, plateauing and decreasing in performance. In the CLA coaching sessions are designed to provide availability of information to be attuned to. The concept of 'repetition without repetition' is a key influencer.

The term 'Perception Action Coupling' is used to show how environments create behaviours and behaviours effect environments. When we move we change the environment before us and therefore the 'affordance' or opportunity for action change. American kinesiologist Karl Newell was one of many to be greatly influenced by Bernstein's work. Newell (1986) proposed that there were three categories of constraints;

- Organism (Individual) Constraints -Physical or mental influences on behaviour. Height, weight, limb length, personality, confidence.
- Task Constraints- Rules of the game e.g. field size, player numbers, number of goals, scoring metrics, equipment etc.
- Environmental Constraints- Environmental factors that surround the players. Temperature, playing surface etc.

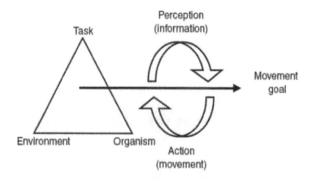

In the CLA, coaches manipulate constraints to allow players become sensitive to them and thereby design a session that is rich in problem solving and genuine learning opportunities. 'Task constraints' are the easiest, most obvious and most effective for coaches to manipulate. We will see how to do this effectively in the next chapter.

And so coaching can be viewed as raising 'in- game awareness' and the Constraints Led Approach is a good way to do this. We want our players to have to continually solve real game problems. This is where the learning is.

What do you see as the advantages to a Constraints Led or Games Based Approach to coaching?

_____

_____

Raising Awareness 'Of-Game' and 'Of-Self'

The Questioning Style

To coach is to 'draw out'. Appropriate use of questioning plays a vital role here. The questioning style lends itself directly to coaching through the Constraints Led or Games Bases Approach. Telling a child something they already know is a lecture that creates disconnection. We must illicit as much as we can thereby raising self-awareness. We must engage them and lead them to learning and awareness. We must challenge appropriately. Many underestimate children (and indeed adult players) and end up in the loop of the famous lecture that nobody really listens to. There is no learning in it. There is no engagement.

Can we ask the children we coach for the solutions before we give them our answers? Can we organise and plan practices that will create problems for them to solve? Can we engage them through questioning and become a child or player centred coach?

Why should the child be at the centre of our coaching?

_____

_____

Observant readers may have noticed, that even in this early part of the book, most of my style has been questioning and eliciting answers. I am coaching you to coach and using questioning as my primary methodology. Some will no doubt feel I have asked too many questions and may have found this irritating or off putting. I would argue that in an exercise such as this the volumes and type of questions are necessary. However, there is learning in this for you. Too many questions, is not the answer.

Using questioning with children is something you must plan and practise. You will have to learn the correct level to pitch your questions at. Below I will share with you a number of ways questioning can be used in a child friendly manner. I will start with basic lower order, closed or convergent, questions which you can use with younger children and then look at some higher order, open or divergent, questions you can use with older child and indeed teens and adults.

(I must clarify that direct instruction still has a place. Non-directive coaching alone does not work and often the level of instruction you need to use can depend on previous knowledge and experience of the children. We have to give them a base line of information to get them up and running).

(Coaching by Contrast) *Right vs wrong*
A problem to solve

When directly coaching basic techniques to young children (5-8 years) I often like to use coaching by contrast. Yes, games are the mainstay of my coaching but there are times when technique must be thought. In short, the further away they are from an acceptable execution of a technique the more direct coaching they need and as the nearer they come to acquire the technique the need for direct coaching decreases.

When used appropriately I feel coaching by contrast is an engaging and effective methodology. It involves giving the children two options, Option A and Option B, two things to compare. Sometimes I will do this visually (coach as demonstrator) and orally and often the examples I use can be total opposites. For example, Option A dribble a ball close to the body using tight control, or Option B dribble a ball with lose control and the children give me the answer (in truth it is a convergent question which leads them to the answer).

An alternative, more player- centred constraints based example, of coaching by contrast could be coaching something like running technique where I would A) ask them to run with their arms behind their back, and B) run with their arms free and loose. I ask them which felt better and then ask; *what do we do with our arms when we run?* They answer and I smile and affirm. It has been 'pulled out' of them.

A final example of coaching by contrast would be doing a tackling exercise where to begin the tackler isn't allowed touch the opponent or the ball. They are left with no option but to move their feet in order to make any impact on the task. In the majority of field sports movement of the feet is key in tackling. By taking the contact out of the tackle and using contrast you are allowing them find the answer. They foundation of good tackling is good footwork. They already have the answer but are unaware they know it. Through contrast we are merely heightening their awareness.

Coaching by contrast is a beautiful child friendly way to coach. Children find it engaging and you are empowering the child and leading them to learning. You are raising their awareness that the answers lie within. You are creating an engaged, self-aware player.

Rate of Perceived Exertion
Another question I like to ask is; how hard are you trying out of 10? (with adults we call it 'rate of perceived exertion' or RPE). Instead of asking them to try harder I am raising their own awareness of how hard they are trying and taking it from there. We want to coach effort and in order to do this we must engage the player. We must challenge them to be the best they can be. Often questions are the answer.

The Spot and Raise Awareness Approach- Coach through Context
The term 'Spot and Fix Approach' is often used in coaching nowadays. I have rephrased it into 'Spot and Raise Awareness'. I feel it's the proper way to look at it. It sets my perspective. It is the ultimate coaching lens. I use it both in endorsing positive actions and skill execution, and addressing coaching opportunities or interventions. The Constraints Led Approach is the platform for this methodology.

For example, if I see a display of beautiful skills being executed in a small sided or modified game, occasionally I can stop the game (if appropriate) for twenty to thirty seconds, the child re-enacts it and we all show our appreciation in a warm manner. These beautiful actions and pieces of skill are happening around us all the time in our coaching. We are building, inspiring and shaping our players through awareness of what's happening in front of us.

In a similar vein, if a child runs into difficulty in a game situation I can stop it momentarily, put them back into the scenario and give them another opportunity to solve the problem. In coaching this is called the 'freeze replay method'. I like to use this technique as I feel it is hugely empowering for the player. Often if assistance is required it comes in the form of the simple question, "What did you see there? What was a better option?" These are 'divergent questions' which are questions which force the player to think. We are using questions to find out what information the players are picking up and if necessary we can start to direct their attention towards more important things. Divergent questions are really good as they require thinking and self-awareness on the player's part. Through your previous (and ongoing) coaching you will have given them the language to answer intelligently.

Also during a game if I notice they are adapted or restricted by the lack of a certain skill I will raise their awareness of this. So for example, if I see they are forced to go to the right hand side because of a weak left hand side and this leads them to turn into trouble I will simple raise their awareness of the need for the left to be strong, the need for total 'adaptability'. I will ask them; "Can you see the need?" Contextualising the need through questioning is a really important concept here. I am not condemning or judging the lack of skill. I am simply leading them to see the value in developing it. It is a 'why moment'. Why they need to go home and practice. I will also always endorse 'adaptability' every time I see it.

What do you think are the benefits of using questioning in your coaching?

_____

_____

Examples of open ended questions to help raise awareness and create the intelligent player

- Skill Execution– How could you/which way ....?
- Time– When could you ...?
- Space – Where could you...?
- Decision– Which option, who and why...?

The Questioning Style- Pre-Game and at Half Time
Questions are more engaging than answers and so the Questioning Style is great before a game, at half time or during any debrief. The famous pre-match team talk is an excellent opportunity to grow and nurture self-aware thinkers and leaders. Why give the answers when often the players already know them? Why not illicit and ask "how are we going to play today?" If you have coached them well you will get words like; discipline, intensity, work rate, honesty, passion, fight, love. Next you would ask them to give you explicit examples of what this would look like. You will get the bones of an excellent team talk. Let them have their input and use their answers. This can be done either directly before the game or in the previous training session. If you do it in the previous training session you can have a poster on the wall on match day with the words they have given you and these words (approximately 3) are the team's compass. An alternative question could be, "how do leaders play the game?" and these qualities are the focus.

What are the advantages of facilitating player input into the pre-match team talk?

_____

_____

The same concept can be used at half time. The following simple questions may be used: What do we need to start doing? What do we need to stop doing? What do we need to continue doing? With regard to a specific play in the game, you could simple ask, "What could we have done differently?".

Learning to ask the appropriate questions is really important.

"Questions are the answer. The better the question the better the answer."

By raising awareness, you are engaging and awakening the player. It is an internal drive not an externally enforced effort. The answers are coming from within which is truly the only way. You are 'drawing out' and self-actualizing the player. This is coaching. The children will grow into the question we ask them and the conversations we have around and with them.

Understand that you must be patient. As with everything in life it will take the children time to grow into this methodology. Awkward silences and rushed generic, non-considered answers can be common at the beginning. Be patient and persevere. If done appropriately over a sustained period, the quality and the delivery of the responses will improve as the self- awareness develops. If necessary, you can have given certain players a heads up beforehand and have given them time to consider their input. Set it up for success. The 'player to coach connection' and the team connection and environment will obviously be a determining factor in the level of the feedback. The starting point is respect. We will look at this shortly.

Practice using questions appropriately. Be aware that we are developing the qualities that will lead them to reaching their playing potential. We are coaching communication, leadership, problem solving, team work, self-responsibility, and self-dependence and so on. We are progressively lessening our importance as coach. Avoid over kill or death by questioning. We will revisit questioning when we look deeper into planning the Constraints Led or Games Based Approach but for now consider the concept of raising awareness and how questions can be used as an engaging methodology.

Quickly jot down some questions you can use in your coaching.

_____

_____

Coaching Cues

Another coaching area which lends itself to the concept of raising awareness is 'coaching cues'. Coaching cues are snippets of task-orientated information, used to teach the player how to perform a task/skill or to draw their attention to the important elements thereof. Successful coaching sometimes depends on the coach's ability to communicate with the player using simple and effective coaching cues. Attentional focus plays an important role in the acquisition of that skill; therefore, emphasising the importance of an appropriate cue. There are two main types of coaching cues'.

- Internal Coaching Cues direct the players to focus their attention on the body movements associated with the skill for example; bend from your hips/ knees/ back. They always refer to a body part or parts. It is believed that internal cues disrupt movement and control because the player has to 'consciously' organise their body. With that said, it is important to acknowledge that this is not to suggest that internal cues are not effective.
- External Coaching Cues direct the player to focus their attention on the movement effect or the outcome associated with the skill. External cue examples include; Push the ground away (when running), get around the ball (when picking it from the ground in Gaelic Football), the perfect 'C' (when practicing the swing in hurling), scratch the clouds (when swinging your hands over head.) They encourage the player to think more about the outcome than the internal actions needed to perform it. Therefore, it is believed that external cues reduce the conscious interference allowing for subconscious 'self-organisation' and leading to enhanced learning and performance. External cues can be sub-divided into three categories, known as the three D's: Distance, Direction and Description. Distance cues being; focusing on an object close or far

away. Direction cues being; more for movement activities like jumping towards. Descriptive cues are often separated into two categories: action verbs (examples: push, punch, punt, drive, cut and explode) and analogies (examples: catch in the basket or slingshot the ball). For the purpose of the book we won't go any further here but appreciate that effective cuing is a very important part of high end coaching.

Raising Awareness of Unsustainable Athletic Based Success
The concept of challenging appropriately is unending but I feel raising awareness of the need to de-emphasize unsustainable athletic based advantage or success is worthy to note in this section. You probably have a number of players who are either really fast, tall, strong etc. Currently they can use this quality to a huge advantage. Over time, the premium on this will erode as teams will figure out how to defend and counteract this or indeed the gap in the physical advantage will probably lesson. You need to teach them not to rely on this physical prowess now, when it helps them look good, at the cost of them not being able to play a more skilled game later. Challenge them appropriately; stretch them. Sometimes it might involve placing them with an older group for a period in order to draw their attention to the challenge. Also, as always, practice design plays a key role in addressing this issue.

Raising Awareness of Home Practice
Systematically and proactively raising awareness of the importance of home practice is another vital area. Deliberate practice is a proven means of improving but this must be pursued in a child friendly age appropriate manner. We will look at this shortly in the research chapter.

Raise Awareness of being a good Team Mate
Raise awareness of what it is to be a good team mate and watch the self-awareness and connection in the team grow. Revisit the section on connection and the team charter.

Raising Awareness among Parents

We have looked at this in connecting with parents but it is important to link it with this topic. Sometimes we have to coach the parents too. In the beginning of year meeting you can repectectfully challenge parents through the use of questioning. Lead them to understanding. Questions like; how does a good parent support their child in sport? What is acceptable and unacceptable behaviour for a parent on the side-line at a game? In the cold light of day, the answers are irrefutable but in the 'heat of battle' people lose the run of themselves. Addressing this at the beginning of year gives you a clear reference point and a common understanding of what is and isn't acceptable.

Feedback Driving Coach Awareness-
Questionnaires and Surveys

There is no such thing as the perfect coach. There is no such thing as the perfect coaching session. Coaching is not a game of perfect. You coach really well some days, other days (indeed months/ years) ...not so much. I am often unhappy with sessions or even groups of sessions over a period of time. This is life, even performance in coaching is nonlinear. The real challenge is can you continue to learn and be true to yourself? Feedback is vital. It improves our perspective and helps us move forward and continue to learn. It stretches us. Welcome and facilitate feedback!

"Feedback gives you new lenses."

Listen to your critics (you will have critics); there is often some element of truth to what they say. You must facilitate feedback and use it to feed forward. Give player (older children) and parent questionnaires and surveys intermittently. Get their insight in your coaching and into the team (again you can get someone to help you with this). It's amazing what you will learn. If you get very few responses it is an indication of a break down in connection. This alone is feedback.

The survey could be as simple as; what do we need to start doing in training? What do we need to stop doing in training? What do we need to continue doing in training? You can also use the 'more of/less of' type angle. Take the useful answers on board. People see things we are often blind to.

"Coaching is not about self-preservation, it's about self-improvement."

Reflection as a tool to Raise Awareness
Reflection will be dealt with in detail later. It is one of the key elements in The CARVER Framework. For now, we will note it as an awareness driver and later we will learn how to plan and practice it.

A Mentor
I must reiterate the value of a mentor. Again we revisit the concept of coaching being a craft. All craftsmen serve their time under a mentor or, if they're lucky, a master craftsman. If you can get someone you know and respect to give you constructive feedback you are on a winner. Alternatively, you could find a professional mentor and invest in your coaching. Their job is to 'draw' or 'pull' the coach out of you.

What might be the benefits of having a coaching mentor?

_____

_____

"Thank You" Raises Awareness
Gratitude is a big buzzword right now. In its simplest form gratitude is merely saying, "Thank you". Everybody must say a simple 'thanks'. For me, it is the child saying, "Thanks Coach, I know you have helped me and I have gained value from attending your training session." The child is acknowledging the good they have received. It is registering with them. It is the coach saying, "Thanks kid, I enjoyed coaching you, we both gained and learned." I also ask them to thank their parents for bringing them to training. If players say thanks consistently their awareness of the value and goodness they are receiving will increase.

Why should all children and coaches practice gratitude?

_____

_____

The Magic Question
The magic question at the end of every session is always, "What did you learn today?" I continuously raise awareness in my players that there are two types of players, learners and non-learners. The question "What have you learned today?" sums up a session nicely. You are testing and coaching at the same time. Again it will take time for the children to become more self-aware and provide more meaningful, considered answers. Be patient.

"Make them aware of their learning"

To end, the coach is constantly looking to raise awareness; 'in game', 'of game' and 'of self'. Don't take yourself too seriously or you will only disconnect yourself from those you are a meant to be coaching. Learn, get a proper perspective and inspire. Your perspective on your role as coach is hugely important.

Summary Points
1. The power, potential and scope of coaching children in sport is huge.
2. Lessons and principles transferable to life should be coached through sport. Raise self-awareness among the children.
3. Know and understand why you are coaching children and why you are coaching them the way you are. Your 'why' drives everything.
4. Know and understand your role as coach.
5. Coach through a Constraints Led or games based Approach. Raise 'in-game awareness'. Coach the game 'out' of them. Understand the role, problem solving has in skilled play and

design your sessions with a view to offering the children multiple opportunities to solve problems.

6. Practice using questions. Raise awareness 'of-game' and 'of-self'.
7. Coach/instruct through contrast.
8. Spot and raise awareness. Coach through context.
9. Use feedback to raise awareness. Questionnaires and surveys will help guide you.
10. Try find a mentor to guide you.

Awareness is key!

Can you see?

CHAPTER 5
RESEARCH

In order to coach well you must; know yourself, know the person/ child and know the sport. Best practice and best principles must be the cornerstone of your coaching and the framework around which you build your 'coaching world'. As coaches we really must move away from working off assumptions. By this I mean assuming what we have done in the past or what you did yourself as a child were the best and only ways. 'What is good for the child is good for the player' is a great lens to look through in your coaching and will drive your desire to learn.

As with everything in life, research is vital. By research I really mean learning the relevant information and having a broad appreciation of best practice and principles. We are not going to go extremely deep here. Heavy research based reading is beyond the scope of what this book is about.

Learning gives us a new perspective. Research on children and skill based performance will develop your coaching eyes. In many ways coaching and sporting performance are learning competitions.

List a set of learning goals for yourself with regard to learning for your coaching. What areas do you feel you need to focus on?

_____

_____

The great coach will continually research new concepts and information. They appreciate how much there is to learn and never think they know it all (or even close). There is honesty and vulnerability to them. In contrast, the greatest obstacle to learning is often the illusion of knowledge. The great coaches will always be looking to hone their craft. The more you know the more you can see and apply. Mastery oriented is what we must be; it's that continuous striving for betterment. It is about planning, practicing, reflecting and learning. That process is where the mastery is. Becoming a better coach is a never ending journey.

Below I have broken down information into different areas I feel the child coach needs to know and research. No area is covered in great detail, or in an overly academic fashion. Again this chapter is not all about hard-core research; but rather the relevant information in what I hope is a clear and useful way.

In coaching you must set everything up for success and you must manage your expectations. Discerning the appropriate challenge by taking the age, development and the ability of the child into account is key. You must know the child. You must know what is in front of you. We meet the child where they are at as opposed to where we want them to be. In order to do this, you must know the basics. Over time you can study different areas in more detail if you wish. We now live in the information age and books, articles, the Internet, YouTube and podcasts are huge resources for coaches.

The Child's Needs

We begin with the child. This is a child-centred philosophy of coaching. There really can be no other way.

"Seek to understand before being understood."

Firstly, we must appreciate that children, like all human beings, have needs. You need to know this and use it to inform your coaching. Our coaching must meet their needs.

The 10 Things Children Need Most
Taken and adapted from *www.cyf.govt.nz*

- Meeting their everyday needs.
- Feel safe and secure.
- Love and hugs.
- Plenty of praise.
- Smiles.
- Talking.
- Listening.
- Learn new things.
- Take care of their feelings.
- Rewards and special treats.

Put simply, children crave; attention, love, learning, acknowledgement and so on. They are egocentric. Children want praise; but please don't confuse this with producing 'praise junkies'. Genuine and specific praise is best (we will see how to do this later). They want to be able to learn and complete a task. They gain confidence through competence and vice versa and this drives them to action. They want to be challenged and engaged. They aim to please.

Children must learn everything as they go through childhood. They need to learn. What we make important they will grow to value as important. They learn so quickly so make sure they are learning well. Regardless of their behaviours outside of coaching time we can coach them to be relatively good learners when they are under our tuition. It is a thing called 'situational behaviour' whereby children learn what behaviours work best in given situations or associate certain behaviours with certain situations. Environment is the hand that guides behaviour.

"If we create the proper environment the desired behaviours will come in time. Be patient."

Keep looking at the needs and ask yourself; are your coaching sessions feeding these needs? Realise and accept that 99% of the time it is not them that are driving you mad; it is you that are driving them mad.

How Children Learn Best- Play and Games

Play is a child's language. Games are the doorway to the child. Children love to play and have fun and must be encouraged and facilitated to continue to do so throughout their childhood (adults should too by the way). Every coaching session must allow the child to be a child. Learning must be made fun; games and play is how we do this. Children learn as they play, and, in play, they learn how to learn.

Children are not young adults and should not be treated or coached as such. Often, as coaches, we leave the fun and play stage of their development behind too early and train them using simpler versions of adult drills. This leads to a non-social, non-stimulating session, unruly and bullying type behaviour, indiscipline, inequality and disrespect within the group environment often leaving the coach powerless and frustrated.

It should be a priority of child coaching to facilitate the child to see out the fullness of their childhood. It is my contention that we are taking children out of their childhood, and thus learning, too early through poor coaching. Every child coaching programme should be developed around play and games and social interaction. Lack of fun is the number one reason children quit sport.

This is not to say there is no purpose only that fun is the priority. Play should have learning consequences. Children will develop physical, social and emotional qualities through fun games and activities, rather than a sole focus on performing traditional skill-based drills in isolation from the game. Research some good games and watch the children develop *(see appendix).* You can also design games and challenges or ask for the children to help you. They will know many games so you can give them ownership of this. Give them autonomy and thereby empower and energise them.

The Child in Sport- Behaviours, Characteristics and Factors to Consider

During childhood the child's developing body and brain alternate between periods of rapid growth and stability. This pattern has significance for coaches. Below are some of the factors that must be considered and appreciated. They are general enough in nature and every group will throw up unique behaviours. Note that as a guide a player can present as plus or minus two years of their chronological age.

Younger Children – 5- 8 years
- They are self-centred and co-operation can be an issue.
- They can struggle with focus and be easily distracted. They will only respond to partner work and skills practice for a short time. They can tire easily.
- They can become upset easily and over- react to in- game contact- 'he/she hit me'.
- A growth spurt happens in the brain of children between the age of 6 and 8 years influencing sensory and motor areas. There is an improvement in fine- motor skills and hand- eye coordination.
- Many think that the ball is their own 'toy' so at times give them all a ball- one ball per child.
- They will only watch the ball and cannot and will not look for space to run into or others to pass to. The beehive effect will be present (all around the ball) in games. As they mature they will begin to see the need to help their teammates and play as a team.
- They usually enjoy being asked questions.
- They respond well to target games, challenges and races. They love games and play.
- Positive and precise feedback is vital. Respect and effort can be ingrained.

- As they mature they will begin to respond to discipline and fairness from the coach. Consistency is key (SAID Principle).

Older Children 9-12 years

- The growth spurt in the brain between the ages of 10 and 12 has most influence on the frontal lobe which is responsible for the cognitive functions such as logic and planning. The player should have a greater 'game' and 'team sense' improving decision-making, information processing and attentional focus. Significant improvement in the player's ability can be apparent as they begin to predict situations better and to find right solution more often and faster. Players begin to show genuine adaptability and compete with greater intensity.
- Weaker players may begin to feel inferior. Many fail to recognise the need to attack the ball and prefer to wait. This needs to be addressed appropriately.
- Groups and cliques can start to emerge. Socialisation is key
- Training needs to moderately increase.
- Players can be graded by ability to ensure the appropriate challenge is forthcoming. This must obviously be done in a fair, transparent and planned manner.

The C's of Success in Sport (and life)

These C's describe the developmental outcomes for children and young people which when achieved seem to facilitate their growth and a positive transition into adult sport and life.

The 4 C's of Athlete Development (Cote and Gilbert 2009)

1. **Competence**– A positive view of one's action in sport.
2. **Confidence**– An internal sense of positive self-worth in sport.
3. **Connection**– Positive bonds with people and institutions in sport.
4. **Character**– Respect for societal rules, integrity, and empathy for others.

5C's model developed by Lerner et al. (2005) and added to by Haskin (2010).

Along with the 4C's of Athletic Development this model added

5. **Caring**–A sense of sympathy and empathy to others and of caring and being cared for.
6. **Creativity**– The ability of the young people to find their own solutions to problems, think for them and think creatively.

When the C's are well developed, a final 'C' emerges. This is the 'C' of 'Contribution' which refers to the fact that children and young people who develop the 'C's' end up making a stronger contribution to themselves, their team and their communities.

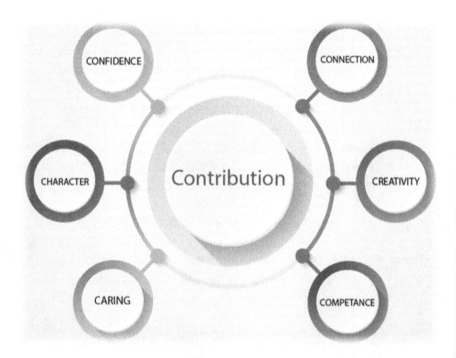

SAID Principle- Specific Adaptation to Imposed Demands

Coaches must consider, understand and appreciate the power of the SAID Principle; Specific Adaptation to Imposed Demands. It is the principle of specificity and consistency. I continually reference it when explaining concepts on improvement and learning.

In simple terms (relative to coaching) it means; "you get what you coach for". The children will grow to be a product of the coaching environment and the demands we place on them within that environment. They will adapt to the demands we place on them over time. Understanding the power of the expanse of time and how we can purposefully create positive adaptations is critical. The law of consistency!

If we purposefully and consistently socialise the children, they will have every chance of being a close and united group. Awareness and a commitment to 'values' will create a healthy sporting environment and healthy sporting children will be the by- product. If we coach them at one speed they will learn to play at one speed. If we coach them in one direction they won't be so good at twisting, turning and changing direction. If we continuously and purposely challenge and stretch them they will grow to be highly adaptable. Consistently provide the specific demands and adaptations will follow.

Nurturing and Supporting Learning

Any philosophy of teaching or learning will show that great teachers teach people how to think not what to think, they facilitate learning, they guide, they engage, they challenge. They raise awareness and open things up for children. Learning is an internal activity, not a spectator sport. Telling someone something is not nearly as effective as leading them to learn and understanding for themselves, heightening their awareness. Information and instruction only is at the lowest level of teaching and coaching.

"Tell me and I forget, teach me and I may remember, involve me and I learn."
Benjamin Franklin-
One of the Founding Fathers of the United States

'Guided Discovery' is a powerful philosophy and concept aligned to the Constrains Led Approach to coaching. We are leading them to learn for themselves through making them an active agent in their own learning. The player is the one driving the process.

One of the world's great Developmental Psychologists, Lev Vygotsky, talked about providing 'scaffolding' for learning. The coach can act as scaffolding for the child to climb up on in order reach new heights. He also talked of a 'Zone of Proximal Development', which is where learning takes place. It is the gap between one's pre-existing ability and what they can accomplish with the appropriate assistance of a 'learned other'.

This chimes nicely with me and sums up coaching pretty succinctly. Coaching a child is all about their learning as opposed to your coaching. Actively work on ways to limit instruction. Too much is counterproductive. Children have an innate drive and need to learn we must nurture it appropriately.

Peer to peer coaching is a beautiful methodology. It works really well when you have slightly older children helping with younger ones. For example, U12's and U11's with U7's and U8's. Using a small sided games model the older children can referee and coach a little with guided supervision from an adult. That what you teach, you learn. For me this is also an excellent culture and leadership exercise.

Mistakes are Learning/Coaching Opportunities

When coaching children in sport there are no mistakes only 'Learning/ Coaching Opportunities'. Good coaches are always alive to these 'Coaching Opportunities'. It takes high levels of self-awareness to effectively incorporate this into your coaching. Failure and mistakes are an integral part of the learning process in both playing and coaching. A simple piece of advice would be not to shoot the learner.

"Don't shoot the learner."

Accept and understand the fact that everyone learns from their mistakes (if they are coached properly) and use it as your "Coaching Lens". Mistakes are feedback, which the child can build upon. They are instructional in nature. The practice environment should be designed with the appropriate amount of challenge present, for the appropriate amount of mistakes to take place, in order for learning to happen. In order to learn they have to fail on a consistent basis.

In truth, an even more appropriate way of looking at it when working with kids would be; they are not making a mistake, they are beginners. Think of the baby learning to walk. There is so much to learn; so much to make unconscious. They learn to hold things. They stand. They fall. They hold things and walk. They fall. They try to walk unaided. They fall. They walk! They fall. They toddle along. They fall. Eventually, they run. They fall. Over the expanse of time they fall less. They need time. Adults challenge and assist them throughout the process and praise their effort: success follows. They simply become more efficient at solving movement problems.

Allow children to fail. It is instructional in nature. Embracing failure leads to experiential learning. Mistakes are happening for the children. Coach this understanding to the children; "Mistakes are happening 'for us' not 'to us'". Raise their awareness of this.

Our job in coaching is to support them through their mistakes. I always explain to the children that;

"The first mistake is ok but the second mistake it not."

It is my way of explaining that they must learn not compound mistakes by making another one straight away. I explore this concept through reference and example e.g. If you miss the ball first time, recover immediately and go for it again straight away, don't give up or foul your opponent. Missing the ball is your first mistake and that's ok, but giving up or fouling is your second mistake and that is not.

Remember the Questioning Style; use open ended questioning to learn from mistakes, a dialogical approach. The right questions will get you the right answers. We are creating a culture of learning, intelligence and problem solving. There are two types of players; a 'Learner' and a 'Non-Learner'. A Learner is the type of player who is continuously striving to learn and improve and accept the latest challenge. Over the expanse of time they reach their potential. We must help lead them to be 'learners'.

If the children, we coach are afraid of making mistakes their development will be stifled. Fear and anxiety will lead to the freezing of the 'degrees of freedom' in the body. We are looking to create an environment of understanding not fear. The more the children understand mistakes the less they fear them. The less they fear them the less they appear. They are free to learn.

Instead of judging a child by their mistakes my motto is:

("Judge Effort First (JEF)")

JEF is a lens I use to view the children I am coaching. Perspective is critical in coaching as we see things as we are not as they are. We really can't ask much more from a child than that they try their best. This is not to say we don't challenge them. We must continuously stretch them. Understanding that mistakes are an integral part of learning and will continue to be minimized and eradicated over the expanse of time if we as coaches promote effort and learning is critical. We must meet the child where they're at as opposed to where we want them to be. The child (and the game) needs time.

Theories and Stages of Skill Acquisition

Skill Acquisition is the study of how we learn or acquire movement skills and sports specific skills. We will look at it in practical terms shortly but for now we will take a brief look at the two main theories or schools of thought behind it. Motor control theories provide us with a base that can lead to effective practice design.

The most accepted theories regarding the stages a learner goes through as they attempt to from go from beginner to expert are one which comes from a more cognitive or behavioural approach and the other which takes a more dynamic systems approach. Appreciating both theories can help any coach understand the nature of the motor learning processes as well as what movement behavioural changes we can expect from the player as they develop.

The most classically popular theory was proposed by Paul Fitts (Fitts & Posner, 1967). It proposes a cognitive theory of skill acquisition that centres on three stages used to explain cognitive and behavioural changes that occur through the learning of skills. Performance is characterized by three stages of learning: the cognitive, associative, and autonomous stages. In the cognitive stage the learner is simply trying to figure out what exactly needs to be done, as well as trying to carry out the performance of it, by identifying the task goals as well as the basic patterns of control and co- ordination. Considerable cognitive activity is usually required. Movements are slow, non-fluid and errors are plenty.

Once the learner has acquired the basic movement pattern, they are thought to have moved to the second, or associative stage of learning. This phase is characterised by subtler movement adjustments and technique improves. The movement is more reliable, relatively more automatic and economical allowing more attention to be directed to other aspects of performance.

As the player moves from the associative stage to the autonomous phase movement and technical execution of the motor pattern has become solidified, fluent and very efficient. They can perform an action without thinking about the execution of the movements involved. A term that you will often hear in association with automaticity is that of "muscle memory" or "motor programs". The skill is performed largely automatically. As attention is no longer occupied by the mechanics of movement it can now be used for improved anticipation and decision-making in multiple scenarios.

Another motor learning thought process has emerged from the ecological psychological theories and comes more from what the learner goes through from a motor systems standpoint or what Nicoli Bernstein referred to as "mastering the redundant degrees of freedom". Carol Newell proposed the model based on Bernstein's perspectives. The three stages of this theory are; Assembling, Control and Optimisation. In the Assembling Phase, the learner will begin to assemble a coordination pattern from the large number of available degrees of freedom in the body. The thinking is the assembling is done by freezing some of the degrees of freedom in order to simplify the movement solution to the motor problem. The joints in the body will be more rigidly fixed.

As the learner begins to feel more in control of the movement they move into the Control Stage. The player begins to unfreeze or reinforce additional degrees of freedom to see can they come up with a more fluid or effective movement pattern and will begin to adapt the motor pattern to the context of the playing environment.

After a significant adjustment period the technical execution will begin to become refined through the degrees of freedom. The stability of that pattern becomes solidified and the player moves into the more optimised skill stage. In this stage control and co-ordination become very refined and efficient.

So which theory is best? Both of the models have merit and can work in conjunction with one another. The 1st (Cognitive/ Assembling), 2nd(Associative/Control) and 3rd (Autonomous/ Optimisation) stages of each of the proposed models correspond to each other. One is cognitive and behavioural and what we are going to see from the learners as they move from beginner level to mastery and in the other we are looking more at how the motor system behaviour will be found corresponding to each stage. The length each learner spends in each stage will be different based on the individual and based on the practise activities the learner participates in as well as a number of other factors. As a rule of thumb players usually spend most time in stage 2.

The Pillars of The Player

Below is some 'needs to know' on what can be termed the 5 Pillars of the Player. I have broken them up into these recognised areas for the purpose of clarity. Each Pillar needs to be nurtured and developed purposely, appropriately and consistently. Can they be developed simultaneously? Yes, and of course they should be is the answer. Are certain pillars more important than other at certain stages in the child's development? Again, yes is the answer. Should we look at them as absolute separates? Maybe yes and no is the correct answer.

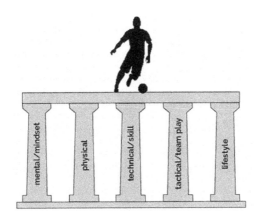

Mental- Mindset

I start with the mental or mindset pillar. Ultimately everything falls unless this pillar is solid and in place. I believe it to be the most essential quality for success in any player. Without it they will not be able to meet the challenges coming to them and never realise their potential. They will be too fragile to be stretched. The mental side of the game is huge and again for me it can be simplified as so, there are two types of children and players: 'learners' and 'non-learners'. Call it what you will; attitude, mentality etc.

Carol Dweck is the lead researcher in this area. Dweck's subject is motivation. She proposes two classes of goals that individuals carry in achievement situations: 'learning goals' and 'performance goals'. Children who strive to learn something new or master a skill are driven by learning goals. Children who are driven by performance goals are preoccupied with their ability and seek to cultivate favourable judgements or avoid negative ones. The learning goal children are interested in increasing their competence. The performance goal children are less likely to accept challenging tasks for fear of revealing inability thereby denying themselves the opportunities to truly learn.

A child who is driven by learning goals will seek challenge and apply themselves to it. If their perceived ability is low, they will choose tasks that promote learning and improvement. If they have high-perceived ability they will accept further challenges in order to improve more. They are less preoccupied with how they will be judged, more willing to display their inability, and they are focused on the process of learning.

Dweck has championed the concepts of 'Fixed' and 'Growth' Mindset. It is a tangible and usable concept. Her book *Mindset- How you can fulfil your Potential* explains it all in detail. Put simply children (and adults) with a Growth Mindset have huge levels of 'coachability'. They just want to learn, they want to be challenged, they want to be stretched. We can, and absolutely must, coach Growth Mindset. Believe me on this or maybe better believe a lady who has devoted her life to it. It's about learning. Learning is a skill. Note: while this article relates to academic pursuits it is fully compatible with sport.

Adapted from Scientific American Special Editions
Volume 23, Issue 5s:

The Secret to Raising Smart Kids
HINT: Don't tell your kids that they are...More than three decades of research shows that a focus on process, not on intelligence or ability, is key to success in school and in life.
By Carol S Dweck

Growing Pains
- *Many people assume that superior intelligence or ability is a key to success. But more than three decades of research shows that an overemphasis on intellect or talent—and the implication that such traits are innate and fixed—leaves people vulnerable to failure, fearful of challenges and unmotivated to learn.*
- *Teaching people to have a growth mind-set, which encourages a focus on process rather than on intelligence or talent, produces high achievers in school, (sport) and in life.*
- *Parents, teachers (and coaches) can engender a growth mind-set in children by praising them for their persistence or strategies (rather than for their intelligence), by telling success stories that emphasize hard work and love of learning, and by teaching them about the brain as a learning machine.*

Two Views of Intelligence
Several years later I developed a broader theory of what separates the two general classes of learners— 'helpless' versus 'mastery-oriented'. I realized that these different types of students not only explain their failures differently, but they also hold different theories of intelligence.

The helpless ones believe that intelligence is a fixed trait: you have only a certain amount, and that's that. I call this a 'fixed mind-set'. Mistakes crack their self-confidence because they attribute errors to a lack of ability, which they feel powerless to change. They avoid challenges because challenges make mistakes more likely and looking smart less so. Such children shun effort in the belief that having to work hard means they are dumb.

The mastery-oriented children, on the other hand, think intelligence is malleable and can be developed through education and hard work. They want to learn above all else. After all, if you believe that you can expand your skills, you want to do just that. Because slip-ups stem from a lack of effort or acquirable skills, not fixed ability, they can be remedied by perseverance. Challenges are energizing rather than intimidating; they offer opportunities to learn.

FIXED MINDSET		GROWTH MINDSET
Something you're born with Fixed	**SKILLS**	Come from hard work Can always be improved
Something to avoid Could reveal lack of skill Tend to give up easily	**CHALLENGES**	To be embraced An opportunity to grow Persevere
Unnecessary Something you do when you are not good enough	**EFFORT**	Is essential The pathway to improvement
Get Defensive Take it personal	**FEEDBACK**	Feedback useful Something to learn from Identify areas to improve
Blame others Get discouraged	**SETBACKS**	Part of learning Necessary for growth

Can you see why mindset is important for the player and can you see why it is important we coach it? Can you see the power, potential and scope of coaching? Can you see why if you value effort and praise the process your players will learn to fly? We will look at this in more detail when we look at 'Endorsing'.

Why is mindset important in a player?

_____

_____

Physical

Physical Literacy
Understanding and appreciating what the child is physically able to do and what is best for them to be doing is massively important in child coaching. It is not all about the ball and the sport. Developing Physical Literacy among the children we coach is one of the greatest gifts we can give the child and the player. What is good for the child will be good for the player, team and the club. Physical Literacy is the mastering of fundamental movement skills and fundamental sport skills that allow the individual to move confidently and with control in a wide range of physical activity situations. It supports long term participation and performance to the best of one's ability.

Internationally recognised Coach and Athletic Development leader Vern Gambetta talks about the body being;

"Connected, linked and synced, to reduce force, produce force or stabilize at the appropriate time in the appropriate plane at the correct time in milliseconds."
Vern Gambetta

Physical Literacy is absolute cohesion in the body, and is a massive determining factor in success in sport and active living. Physical Literacy develops a 'movement vocabulary' of Fundamental Movement Skills (FMS) and fundamental sports skills. It is the ABC's of movement: Agility, Balance, Coordination and Speed.

Ask yourself; how much physical activity and opportunities to develop athleticism are there in your current average training session? Are the children moving at a snail's pace after a ball? Are there periods of vigorous physical activity in your training session? Are the children being physically challenged?

Now ask yourself what physical qualities will the child require to have a reasonable chance at successful long term participation in the sport? Be aware of where you are trying to bring them, your vision. Have a 'future focus'. Future focus means understanding and appreciating that it is our job is to prepare the child for 'what is yet to come'. We ultimately want them playing at high intensity, fast and aggressive. If they don't have the physical foundation to do this, they won't be able to keep up with what you're asking them to do. Our job is development.

I am not any way anti ball skills or ball based games (how would I be?) but I believe sole focus on the ball in children's training sessions can limit the opportunity to develop athletic qualities in the child which will be invaluable to them as they move on in their chosen sport. Physically literate children make better sports people. Every sports-specific action or posture demands that the player has an appropriate level of movement efficiency to carry out the task. You are purposefully taking them 'off the ball' in order to keep them 'on the ball' long term, although it must be noted that the ball can often be incorporated in an innovative, non-traditional manner.

When training children it is worthwhile to strategically leave aside the ball and the highly technical skill-set required to play the given game and develop the FMS (and of course other non-physical qualities) through a variety of play based games *(see appendix)*.Physical literacy games develop athletic qualities and abilities through creating scenarios which challenge the child's movement in relation to the activities of others which is ultimately what we are trying to achieve in the actual game we coach.. In other words; these games are representative and couple perception and action. The movement skills are being developed and learned implicitly. It is guided discovery through play and games.

What are Fundamental Movement Skills (FMS)?

Fundamental Movement Skills (FMS) are movement patterns that involve different body parts. They are the foundation movements or precursor patterns to the more specialised, complex skills used in various sports. It is the development of this movement vocabulary upon which we build the sports specific techniques and postures.

There are three widely accepted categories of FMS and they are loosely listed below

Body Management Skills	Locomotor Skills	Object Control Skills
1. Rolling	1. Crawling	1. Throwing
2. Stopping	2. Running	2. Catching
3. Bending	3. Galloping	3. Striking
4. Twisting	4. Walking	4. Bouncing
5. Landing	5. Hopping	5. Dribbling
6. Stretching	6. Skipping	6. Kicking
7. Climbing	7. Dodging	
8. Balancing		
9. Turning		

Why is it Important we coach Fundamental Movement Skills to children?

- There is a strong correlation between those high in FMS competency and long term physical activity. FMS form the building blocks for sport specific skills.
- An emphasis on FMS development will produce athletes who have better trainability for long-term sport-specific development.6- 10 years old is optimum time to develop FMS.

- FMS can and in my opinion should be developed in a game and play based environment, therefore we can use FMS games as an opportunity to socialise the group.
- Children need to develop FMS before they can effectively learn Sport Specific Skills. Sports Specific Skills (SSS) are these movement skills applied to a sporting situation, for example, kicking a soccer ball, running a sprint, jumping up for a basketball rebound, catching a football etc. If we place a heavy emphasis on sport skills before movement skills, children will struggle to learn the sport skills or at least won't master them to as high a level as they could have. We must understand that players need the physical competencies to do the sports skills. With older players, complex movements are hard to coordinate if they haven't mastered the foundational movements.

(*ADAPTED) YOUTH PHYSICAL DEVELOPMENT MODEL FOR MALES

AGE (YRS)	4	5	6	7	8	9	10	11	12
GROWTH RATE	RAPID	< > STEADY GROWTH				< > ADOLESCENT SPURT			
MATURATIONAL STATUS	PRE-PHV							< PHV	
TRAINING ADAPTATION	PREDOMINANTLY NEUTRAL < >					NEUTRAL & HORMONAL < >			
PHYSICAL QUALITIES	FMS	FMS				FMS	FMS	FMS	
	SSS	SSS				SSS	SSS	SSS	
	MOBILITY	MOBILITY							MOBILITY
	AGILITY	AGILITY							AGILITY
	SPEED	SPEED							SPEED
	POWER	POWER							POWER
	STRENGTH	STRENGTH							STRENGTH
			HYPERTROPHY						HYPERTROPHY
	E & MC		ENDURANCE & MC						
TRAINING STRUCTURE	NONE	LOW					MODERATE		

PRE-PHV (PEAK HEIGHT VELOCITY)

FMS (FUNDAMENTAL MOVEMENT SKILLS)

SSS (SPORT SPECIFIC SKILLS)

ENDURANCE & MC (METABOLIC CONDITIONING)

BOLD - INDICATES IMPORTANCE

(*ADAPTED) YOUTH PHYSICAL DEVELOPMENT MODEL FOR FEMALES

AGE (YRS)	4	5	6	7	8	9	10	11	12
GROWTH RATE	RAPID < >		STEADY GROWTH		< >		ADOLESCENT SPURT		< >
MATURATIONAL STATUS	PRE-PHV			<		PHV		< >	
TRAINING ADAPTATION	PREDOMINANTLY NEUTRAL			< >		NEURAL & HORMONAL			< >
PHYSICAL QUALITIES	FMS	FMS			FMS			FMS	
	SSS	SSS			SSS			SSS	
	MOBILITY	**MOBILITY**						MOBILITY	
	AGILITY	**AGILITY**						**AGILITY**	
	SPEED	**SPEED**						**SPEED**	
	POWER	**POWER**						**POWER**	
	STRENGTH	**STRENGTH**						**STRENGTH**	
	E & MC		HYPERTROPHY	ENDURANCE & MC			HYPERTROPHY	ENDURANCE & MC	**HYPERTROPHY**
TRAINING STRUCTURE	NONE	LOW						MODERATE	

PRE-PHV (PEAK HEIGHT VELOCITY)

FMS (FUNDAMENTAL MOVEMENT SKILLS)

SSS (SPORT SPECIFIC SKILLS)

ENDURANCE & MC (METABOLIC CONDITIONING)

BOLD - INDICATES IMPORTANCE

These graphs must be qualified by the fact that children have unique developmental differences. These include the rate of development in skills between individuals and between skills. A child may be at mature levels in some skills and at initial in others.

Incorporating Physical Literacy into our Coaching Sessions
Children do not develop automatically in physical literacy and this is an ever-increasing fact in today's sedentary, health and safety conscious child rearing era. Children simply aren't moving as much anymore. The need for coaching FMS is now greater than ever and I would predict it will continue to increase.

When coaching a sport there is the danger that the technical skills and demands of the sport will by and large take precedence. Again, I urge you to consider the perils of letting the sport get in the way of what is good for the child.

"The critical, fundamental phase is often overlooked by coaches, teachers and parents, who focus on competition and winning rather than the acquisition of basic skills and fitness."
Istvan Balyi-
Internationally recognised Expert in Long Term Athlete Development

We are currently taking children at a younger and younger age into organised sport. Perhaps before they are developmentally ready for the demands of the sport or perhaps more accurately, before we, as coaches, are equipped or skilled enough to coach a child of that age. If we get it wrong, I believe this practice is more counterproductive than we appreciate. If we take a child at say six years of age (or indeed up to eight) we need to appreciate that there is still a number of years to go before they are even out of childhood. Four or five years of poor, non-child-centred, non-age appropriate coaching is a huge missed opportunity to 'draw out' physical and athletic qualities. The foundation hasn't been built with purpose and care.

A question I often ask clubs and coaches is "What are the physical qualities you wish to see in your adult players?" They invariably say things like "speed, agility, strength, power, flexibility." The basis for these psychical qualities is developing physical literacy through practising and improving FMS and it is self-evident that we should be systematically developing physical literacy. For me the best way to do this is to incorporate FMS games into our coaching sessions. If we choose our games wisely *(see appendix)* and coach well, we can also develop a ton of non-physical qualities that will actually help them to be better players and all round happier and healthier people.

If you want to create a comprehensive movement vocabulary then consider; walking, running, skipping, galloping, jumping, bounding and hopping. Factor in direction; forward, backward, sideways, circular clockwise and anti-clockwise. Vary starting position; stationary facing forwards/backwards/ sideways, standing on one foot, kneeling, sitting, lying prone, lying supine, lying on side, on hands and feet prone (4-point), on hands and feet supine (4-point), 3-point and 2-point. Add all of these to relay races, challenges and 'tag' games. 'Gamify' if you can. This gives you; speed and change of direction, perception and action coupling and much more. For me, games and challenges are always a more powerful coaching tool than traditional drills. If you can 'gamify' the development of physical literacy, then I believe this is the way to go. However, it must also be acknowledged that athletic type drills using mini hurdles, cones and poles have their place.

Instruction and Cuing
With regard to actual coaching of the movements, by all means you can intervene and use some instruction and coaching cues. When we first learn a motor skill, all performers need some feedback and instruction. By giving instruction, cues and feedback initially there are fewer errors in these first stages of learning. The fewer the errors, the more confident the learner can be. It is useful to know the coaching cues *(see appendix).*

The Need for Speed
When coaching children, we need to be serious about speed. The first 'critical period of speed development' occurs between the age of 6-8 for girls and 7-9 for boys. Linear, lateral and multi-dimensional speed and agility should be developed and the duration of the repetitions should be less than five seconds. We want our kids running and moving at top speed.

Promoting Multi-Sport Participation.
As part of their developing of physical literacy children should and must be encouraged to play multiple sports. All sports contribute to the acquisition of related FMS and physical competencies. Some sports, such as athletics, martial arts, gymnastics and swimming develop certain skills, qualities and attributes that perhaps team sports do not.

Early specialisation in the vast majority of team sports is totally counterproductive. This is well recognised internationally and early specialisation is now seen a growing problem. As a child coach you must actively promote and support multi-sport participation in the children you coach. It is in their best interests both as a child and a player.

What do you see as the advantages of purposefully developing Physical Literacy in the children you coach?

_____

_____

What are the physical qualities you wish to develop in your players?

_____

_____

Technical- Skill

I stand firm on my philosophy that how we coach the skills of the game should look and feel like the game where at all possible and that the rules and conditions that underpin these games should be tailored to the level of the players in front of you. As we have seen in our chapter on 'awareness' this pedagogy is known as a Constraints Led Approach (CLA) where practice design or training is said to be representative. Again, without being too precious or precise, for the purpose of this book, I will use the terms CLA, Games Based Approach and Conditioned Games Approach interchangeably. I will aim to give you an overview of the area and my hope is that I can provide a fair insight which will be usable and thought provoking for all.

To begin with we must establish an appreciation of what is a skill and what is it to be skilful. We must understand and appreciate that a technique is not a skill. It can be said that a skill is a technique applied to a game where there is perception or decision-making. It is an emergent behaviour in response to what happens around you. Players are not skilful if they can perform techniques in isolation. They are genuinely skilful if they can adapt these techniques to solve and overcome the challenges that appear 'in-game'. Being truly skilful is knowing; what to do, when to do it and how to do it. The challenge for coaches is to design training activities that involve game-like scenarios to promote skill development, while promoting an environment that also develops player confidence.

In a Games Based Approach to coaching you will have more games than drills. The primary focus is on guided discovery, implicit learning and problem solving in a game context. Especially in youth players, self-discovery and problem solving are crucial for their cognitive growth on the field of play. The skills of the game are largely acquired and developed through playing the game itself or a modified version of the game. However, game based does not necessarily mean games only. There is a continuum. At the opposite end of the full on-game it can simply mean bringing an element of variability to a drill or gamifying the drill to a degree.

The Games Based Approach allows for the frequent recurrence of the same basic game situations and requires players to experiment with different solutions and emergent behaviours until some level of mastery and understanding is gained. We are almost stripping it back to the way children learned it in the past when children played on the street or in the garden with their friends (an increasingly rare occurrence nowadays). The Game Based Approach leads to technical proficiency, tactical adaptability, improved decision making and competitive skilled players. Questions can be used to probe and deepen understanding 'of the game'. The 'freeze replay method' can be used as an aid to learning (see previous chapter).

Understanding complex ball sports can best be achieved through the practise of a logical progression of small-sided simplified or modified games, with a gradual increase in team numbers and complexity. As young players are growing physically and mentally, the difficulty and complexity of the simplified games should increase. Creativity is key in session design. Can you design a game or a challenge that meets the child where they're at and brings them to where you want them to be? Can you regress and simplify the demands of the game enough so the child can be competent enough to gain confidence through playing it? If the game has too much complexity or chaos in it the children won't be able to process the volume of information. Set it up for success. To begin, ensure children don't require a high level of ability or specific game knowledge to enjoy and compete in the game. Like everything, designing games takes practice and to truly coach a constraints led approach requires a deep understanding of the underpinning principles and design considerations. We will look at this shortly.

A basic rule is to start simple and small, and progressively make the game more complex as the children progress. The changes can be subtle, add a simple rule, change a simple variable and observe what effects it has. Tasks can be simplified by using various sized equipment for example in indoor hurling you can go from a balloon, to a first touch ball, to a soft touch. This is known as 'task simplification'.

The coach must have patience. Sometimes it won't be pretty, in fact it will most likely be ugly, but there will be rich learning. Understand and appreciate that learning, retention and transfer in a games based training session can be good but performance appear poor. While alternatively, especially in a drill based linear approach, performance in a practice session can appear good but learning, retention and transfer be relatively poor. In other words, coaches who focus on drill based work can run sessions where performance looks great but there may not be huge amount of learning or transfer to game performance because their session is totally removed from the context of the actual game.

"What we learn to do we learn by doing and by being afforded the opportunity to do badly."

They want to play games so play games with them because long-term devotion to training and practice is necessary for their development. Small sided conditioned and adapted games are key. It can be as simple as 1 v 1 or 2 v 2. The technical skills of the game are learned implicitly through playing the game. We are coaching the game 'out of them' not 'into them'.

"Coach the game 'out of them' not 'into them."

Frequent execution of the same techniques or skills (repetition without repetition) stimulates the acquisition and execution of the skills. Perception and action are coupled. The game is being replicated. Everything is happening in context. The reduced numbers and conditions demand that the less-skilled players become centrally involved in the game and give each child the chance to play a genuine role in the game; a real opportunity to improve. The essential aspects of team communication and co-operation between players are also being facilitated and nurtured. Appropriate questioning is used to stimulate learning and raise awareness. Coaching and learning is taking place.

Focusing on Technique

The sport specific skills of the game you coach are vital. One thing I have learned is that if habits create the future then certainly time magnifies flaws. While more and more we have come to appreciate that there is no such thing as perfect technique it cannot be denied that there are minimum technical parameters for the skills of a game. Some take the games based approach as being 'games only' however I feel this isn't necessarily the case. For me, game based doesn't mean that you don't coach technique. It means that you coach it within the context of the game as much as is possible or optimal.

Can they hold the hurl properly? Do they catch the ball properly? Is their running technique efficient? Is coach intervention necessary, beneficial and appropriate? These are question we must be asking. With this noted we must appreciate and understand that all sporting techniques require defined physical qualities for them to take place correctly and developmentally some children might not be there yet.

If you observe, in game, a technical deficiency that is limiting the children's playing capacity or recurring mistakes you can always stop the game, intervene and do a quick appropriate technical activity on the pitch before you resume the game (a play zone activity- we will see this shortly). This is your cue to show the children they need to go home and work on the skill. You are attaching that poor execution of a technique/ skill to a 'why moment' in the context of the game. You are working backwards by starting with the game. This can be known as a Whole- Part- Whole Approach which we will see shortly.

From my point of view, you will focus on technique in isolation only when it improves the game or the ability of an individual to access or play the game. In order to do this, you must know the key points- KCP's and coaching cues (revisit coaching cues) of the skills. KCP's are the steps involved in performing the technique, however they are not to be delivered in such as explicit step by step manner. This is where cuing comes in as well as designing fun tasks and challenges that engage the child and lead them to learning the technique. You must be able to observe and intervene when necessary. You must know the progressions, regressions and interventions in order to provide the appropriate assistance and design tasks and challenges accordingly. You can break down the technique for the child especially at a younger age but you must know how to do so in a fun engaging way. You must meet the child where they are at, not where you want them to be at.

Begin with the child. What part of the skill can they do? Next look at what they need to do. Now intervene and feed them that single piece of information or cue. Let them play with it. Be extremely patient. The learning is in the struggle. Endorse effort. Don't try to force it; facilitate it over time. You may think they 'have it' because they do it for you within a short time frame or there is an acute change in behaviour. This is a practise effect. It doesn't really last. A learning or performance effect is a long term recognisable change in behaviour and that is what we are looking for.

Learn the regressions, progressions and the KCP's and cues of the skills you are trying to coach so you can intervene properly when necessary. Work on designing tasks and challenges to facilitate implicit learning. You are trying to draw the children's attention or awareness to something specific but not in an overly explicit manner.

(See appendix examples of Key Coaching Points)

List the top 5 skills performed in the sport you coach and either research or come up with you own Key Coaching Points and Coaching Cues for each skill.

_____

_____

_____

_____

Whole-Part–Whole-The Play Zone Approach to Coaching Sport Specific Skills

I like a mix of the Games Based Approach and what I call the Play Zone Approach and feel the two complement each other beautifully. In truth, they are similar in concept so we could go directly from playing a game to a quick practice of a technical skill on the pitch (or section thereof, which is used as the play zone) and back to a game.

I am not a huge fan of the traditional 'out to the cone and back' linear drills. I feel they are not a very engaging or effective methodology and neglect the active role of the game environment which shapes movement, perception, cognition and decision making. A more unstructured practice environment provides the necessary ingredients that fulfil all the requirements for children's skill development. Where appropriate I believe in a 'one ball per child' approach and marking out a simple play zone. The size and dimension of the playzone can vary depending on the activity or conditions you want to create or the skill you are focusing on. In the playzone the children are free to travel in any direction while practicing the skill. It must be noted, that you will still have to challenge the players and raise their awareness of the need for; multi directional movement, finding space in the playzone and where appropriate, timing and judging their runs so they come onto the ball at the correct angle, time and speed.

The play zone is dynamic, unpredictable and constantly changing environment like the game they are preparing to play. Modifications and conditions can be added to the challenge. The player will have to adapt accordingly. Embrace the randomness and mess of the play zone. This is how they learn.

I believe you must create a need for what you are trying to coach and it is then we can justifiable challenge to the task at a high level of engagement. Recently I observed a coaching session where the children were doing a linear passing drill from Cone A to Cone B. All the coach kept shouting at them way. "Call his name, call his name." The passer and the receiver were running towards each other while looking directly at each other; a linear drill. There was 'no need' to call a name therefore the coach had to keep asking for it. Calling the name was serving little or no purpose so it can be argued that unconsciously the coach is belittling the intelligence of the player. For me I believe that long term this will lead to a breakdown in the connection between the player and the coach. Now if this skill was coached within a play zone with groups of say a 2 to 1, or 3 to 1, child to ball ratio, where the task was; child 1 passes to child 2, who passes to child 3, who passes back to 1 and so on., there would be a need to call a name, i.e. passer or receiver would have to attract attention of the other due to the chaos created by the other groups intermingling. This is not to say the coach won't need to challenge the children to call out names but rather that the children will grow to have an appreciation of the need to call a name because it is context dependent. They would also soon learn the need to look up and make a clear decision on when and how to pass as again the complex and chaotic nature of the play zone would challenge them to. Sometimes we have to tune their attentional focus or awareness to this fact. As an interesting aside it can be an idea in play zone based activities and games to add a condition that no one is allowed to talk or make noise. In some way this is coaching by contrast but what it really does is force the player in possession to develop their visual processing skills as they can longer utilise their audio skills. You will physically notice them looking around and scanning when this condition is placed on the activity. The coaching is providing the need.

As far as I am concerned most Sports Specific Skills can be coached very effectively in a play zone style. If necessary, it gives you the opportunity to intervene directly on a one to one basis. In this dynamic environment we can: Spot and Raise Awareness- 'the freeze replay method', Coach by Comparison- Give them options A or B, Coach by Constraint, Coach by Questioning, coach directly when needed and teach the Key Coaching Points using a questioning style or appropriate cues.

(See appendix for a systematic approach to coaching skills in the play zone).

Factors to consider in a Games Based Approach

- **Number of Players**

A general rule with children is to keep the numbers small. Currently the mainstream invasion games are accepting children into their clubs at the age of five or six. 1 v 1 or 2 v 2 games work very well here. At that age, the only skills they are ready to develop are dribbling (or the sporting alternative) and scoring (shooting) skills. This fits with the psychological and mental capability profile of these young children, who are very egocentric. They aren't able to deal with complex decision making required to know when to dribble and when and whom to pass. The high level of complexity of the full form of the game doesn't fit with the cognitive capacities of an Under 6 and even some Under 7 or 8 players. We must focus on the development of skills that suit where they are mentally and cognitively, like keeping the ball, running with the ball and scoring.

As they get older we can gradually increase the numbers but always remember small-sided games mean higher player activity, or more repetition without repetition.

"We won, but so what? When (s)he only touched the ball 3 times today. Our responsibility is development. So we must play 4 v 4 or 7 v 7 with plenty of time and space to learn combinations, skills, awareness and smartness."
Rinus Michels- Father of 'Total Football'

- **Dimensions/Size of the Playing Area and Goal-to-Goal Orientation**

Again, starting with young children, to begin, I think it can be absolutely fine to simply put down two cones and let them play away towards the same goal. Taking into account the profile of the player I see this as a perfect starting point for some. Sometimes with young children they find it easier to play towards one goal; one v one (or 2v 2, 3 v 3) into the same goal and side-lines may not even be necessary. Open space can work perfectly. You can also alter and manipulate the direction or location of where the ball in coming from i.e. outwards from the goal or inwards towards the goal from a point out the field. As they mature and develop, side-lines can be introduced as can goal-to-goal orientation.

As regard the size of the playing area it is ok to start with what you think and monitor or reflect on it after each practice. Trial and error can work if you understand and appreciate that children need relatively more time and space on the ball than adults due to their beginner skill level. Sometimes with children we make the pitch too small.

Without doubt they do need space but when the ball isn't travelling long distances due to the beginner skill level we get the 'beehive effect'. It is a difficult one to overcome. As a guideline, as the child get older you can calculate player area by dividing the square meter of the standard adult playing field by the total number of players on the field. That will give you squared meters per player. Again, alternatively you can use a trial and error method once you understand what you are trying to achieve and are diligent enough to reflect and learn as you go

- **Duration of Game**

I feel as the children get older it is a good idea to put a set time limit on a game. Do we always need to do this? No is definitely the answer, but as the children mature setting a time frame on the game can give clarity to the challenge. Over time, this can improve and develop in-game focus and engagement and we can purposely and strategically stretch them by extending the duration of the game gradually.

A general guideline would be that consistently setting and keeping time limits adds focus and drives application. It makes the challenge clear e.g. "I want you to give your best effort for 8 minutes and then we'll take a quick break". Start with what you think appropriate and monitor, reflect on it after each practice; trial and error. Different groups and individuals will have higher application thresholds.

- **Rules, Refereeing and Consequence**

As the children get older it is important that they learn to follow the rules of the game. Do we need to blow the whistle and stop the game for every minor misdemeanour? For me the answer is definitely; No! Some will argue that letting the game flow will feed and lead to poor habits. I believe that in many situations you can referee 'on the fly' and so lessen the need to keep blowing the whistle (i.e. call the free but keep playing).

For me too much refereeing interference sanitizes the game too much for the children and strips it of its joy, energy and excitement. We must appreciate that the children are only learning the skills of tackling and so it is unfair to expect them to be excellent at it or indeed anywhere close. Afford them the opportunity to learn and develop these skills in an engaging environment, not in a stop start game of utter frustration.

With this noted I do believe to add clarity to the challenge it can be important to follow the rules pretty strictly, thereby adding consequence to actions. Consequence is a good way to learn. For example, if the ball crosses the side-line in most circumstances we should call a line ball. If the ball goes wide of a defender call a corner or a 45m free or the equivalent. Being consistent in your application of the rules is not the same as nit picking or being whistle happy. Of course there will be occasions when you ref on the fly or ad hock but by and large consistency is important. Making the challenge clear and adding consequence drives engagement and application over time. It helps to 'draw' out the competitor. Think the SAID Principle.

- **Keeping Score- Scoring Zones or Scoring Metrics**

Again with 'younger children' this isn't really important but as the children get older, perhaps from 9 or 10 years onwards I feel it begins to become more important to keep scores. Having fair and even teams is vital as is the playing environment and culture. We are not tracking scoring to make it a 'win at all costs' or 'winner gets bragging rights' type scenario. We are tracking scores to make the challenge real, to drive application and drive healthy competition, to breed sporting competitors. All of these ingredients add true joy to the game. Players play on the edge and this is where they learn and grow to love the game. It helps to 'draw out' the competitor in them. If you are on the losing side, so be it. Learn how to be a good loser. Learn how to learn from losing. Learn that we are either losing or we are learning and if you are learning you can't lose. Develop resilience, character and self-awareness. Note the playing environment and culture must be spot on in order for score keeping to be an effective learning tool. Depending on the game you can score various elements; we will see this on our section on shaping the game.

- **Captains and Leaders**

As the children grow older it can be a good idea to appoint team captains for training games. They can be given the task of lining out the team, managing and delivering team talks and half time breaks. This player centre strategy facilitates peer-to-peer coaching, as well as the development of leadership qualities and helps produce self-reliant players. Rotate the responsibility among the players over time. Give them ownership of the game.

- **Make Believe Scenarios**

When playing games with children it can be a great idea to create make believe scenarios. For example, in soccer; Man United are 1- 0 down against Liverpool with 5 minutes to go. One team is Man United and the other team is Liverpool. The children can pretend to be various players if they wish e.g. Mo Salah. By adding the extra variable of Man United needing to score you are creating a team challenge for both teams to deal with.

Young children absolutely love this. It adds huge excitement and drives them to truly engage with the make believe scenario in front of them. The coach can act as commentator; adding to the excitement and atmosphere. When done properly player engagement will be sky high.

- **Coaching Assistance**

For small-sided games based model you will obviously need help, we will look at this the section on 'Collective Cohesive Coaching'.

- **Underpinning Values**

We will see this in our section on 'Values'. The values we promote through the game are the absolute driving force of performance and application. They guide the attitude, culture and mindset. They underpin the whole thing. I really cannot over- emphasise the importance of this. This environment and spirit within which the games are played are far more important than the games themselves.

Designing a Constraints Led Approach (CLA)- Shaping the Game

Here to fore we have kept it very simple and gone with a 'when in doubt play a game or gamify a drill' approach and this really is your starting point. Now we will briefly look at how we can intelligently manipulate task constraints to strategically stretch and develop the player. Intelligent and strategic manipulation of 'task constraints' can help develop or 'pull out' certain qualities in the player. If we are looking to take our coaching to the next level we need to look at design features or principles of the C.L.A.A coach must develop the ability to foresee all probable challenges the game can bring, reconstruct them in a training environment, and if needs be assist the player in the problem solving process.

Once again 'affordances' are opportunities for action within the environment or possibilities offered by the environment that can be acted upon e.g. a gap between two defenders or a two on one situation. Helping players become 'attuned to the affordances' is our coaching challenge. We can create sessions and design games that provide availability of specific information to be attuned to. In order to achieve this, we manipulate informational constraints.

The key in the CLA (in its purist sense) is that the 'task constraints' don't specify the exact pattern or skill that has to (or indeed can't) be used. We are seeking to promote and develop 'emergent decision making' not to prescribe the action or give the answer. So if we were looking to quicken up the speed of passing in say Gaelic football a conditioned game like 'No Hop- No Solo' is not the CLA in its purist sense. Providing the answer, or prescribing the solution, is not promoting an 'emergent decision'. You are removing the key triggers and cues from that decision. Ultimately we want to give players autonomy to search for relevant affordances. A better alternative would be to give more passing options by having say 1 or 2 'floater players' that play with the team in possession. In this way you are encouraging quicker movement of the ball in a non-restrictive or prescriptive manner. You are 'offering' or 'heightening the opportunity' in a way that is representative of the game because sometimes the right option will be to hold onto the ball and take the hop or solo. I am not saying there is anything 'wrong' with a no hop no solo rule condition I am just saying that if we can find a truer alternative then this is definitely a positive.

Another example of the CLA would be how we can manipulate scoring metrics to promote certain skills. For example, if you trying to promote high catching in hurling you could add it to the scoring in the game. A high catch could be worth the same as a point. Also, if you were trying to promote width in attack in a game you could set up a scoring gate near each side-line and each time they pass or carry the ball though them it would be a score (say a ½ point so not as to put it on the same footing as a real point/ goal) In this way you are not telling them they have to carry it through the gates before they can attack but you are encouraging them to do it when it is the correct decision to do so.

You are aiming to heighten their awareness of this aspect of the game in a non-prescriptive manner. You are manipulating constraints to 'pull out' various qualities or develop various skills in the player. The challenge for the coach is to develop the ability to design the optimal challenge.

To end I will urge you to allow time for these modified games to develop. It will take them time to figure out the problem the game is posing or the affordances it is offering. You must be patient. It will look ugly and frustrating to begin with but this is where the learning is. The values you promote must fuel the application to the challenge. Finally return to the game at a later date, possibly the next session and allow the children the opportunity to start at a higher level.

Relay Races
Relays are an excellent way of blending social, physical and skill work and creating a challenging competitive environment. Competition is healthy, children love relays. Be creative; use a variety and mixture of

FMS and sports specific skills. Make them fun. You can incorporate obstacle course type activities as well as overlapping pathways, which will incorporate perception and action coupling. Remember relays do not need to be linear (straight line) in nature. They offer huge scope for movement diversity. Ask for the children's input. Using something like a cup of water over the head adds an extra dimension of fun to them. Be sure the children respect the race and follow the rules. Provide fairness and clarity to the challenge. If some don't respect the rules and aren't held accountable the others will lose interest and become demotivated. Respect is at the cornerstone of everything we do.

Tactical- Team Play

As we have seen in our section on building the technical or skill pillar we really must embrace a Games Based Approach to coaching the technical skills and the tactical or team play in tandem. You cannot separate the technical skills from the team play. Without each- other they serve no purpose, therefore you must train them conjointly. Without a purpose any action could be considered unnecessary and if children feel something is unnecessary they won't embrace it or engage fully with it. Proper implementation of the games based approach will throw up all the team play scenarios you could wish for and the questioning style will help lead the children to learn. An over-structured, over-emphasis on tactics too early in the child's development can stifle skill development as well as taking the joy and fun from the game. An emphasis on ball mastery and a general understanding of the underpinning concepts of the game itself, not a specific system, opens up a much larger range of tactical possibilities long term. Tactics will change but the general skill set required to apply them will not. Coaches must have a 'future focus'. My view is that tactics in child sport are best thought of as a means to establish a general understanding and awareness 'of the game' and team play early, thus allowing for a much larger range of tactical possibilities later in a player's development.

Principles of the Game

For me, coaching the tactical or team play side of the game with children centres on the Principles of the Game. We must appreciate that problem-solving, decision making and team work are dependent on background knowledge. The game is about learning to react to cues and read patterns. Therefore, players have to be able to understand some principles of the game in order to be able to access it at a meaningful and logical level. This is your 'of game awareness'

Utilising the games based approach, you can begin to slowly and purposefully introduce these principles as the children mature. They are a unifying concept, acting as information organisers that provide logic or rationality to what we are trying to achieve so that we can work together. Team sports are group problem solving activities. Ultimately we want to create a team that is 'attuned' to 'shared affordances' and therefore it seems logical to provide them with principles they can work off; a common understanding of the game. Principles are few and can be used as a concrete reference or framework to assist in coaching the game. They help my Spot and Raise Awareness Approach. As far as Hurling and Gaelic football (and indeed most invasion sports) are concerned, for me the Principles of the Game can be broken up in to; Principles of Possession, Principles of Support, Principles of Defence and Attack and The Principles of Tackling. I use these principles to diagnose, question and raise awareness. They also provide a shared vocabulary and a common framework for the group.

Principles of Possession- Movement, Vision, Decision, Execution ('Move, Look, Decide, Do')

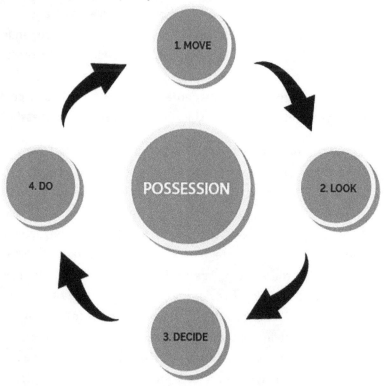

Possession equates to control. The value of possession must be understood and appreciated. The objective must always be to maximise possession. You can't play the game without the ball. For this reason, possession is such a key component and is a central principle of the game. Raising awareness of the importance of possession is vital it will lead them to value and respect it. It doesn't become possession until its value is understood.

1. Movement- Upon gaining possession, did they move (where and why)? If they did move; great! It is the movement that creates the instability or problem for the defender. If they didn't move, we have diagnosed a problem to which we must find a solution. Awareness is the beginning of this. I have

movement in before vision because currently I feel it's a better approach. I want to raise awareness that you get it and move, and then look. You find with kids and adapted adult players: they get it, stand up, look and get swallowed up in the tackle. Eventually you want them looking and moving in tandem and ultimately, looking and scanning before they actually gain possession. Later on; where to move to and why, can be explored again within the context of the game.

2. Vision-Did they look? If they did, great! If they didn't we have diagnosed a problem to which we must find a solution. Awareness is the beginning of this. Once again, ultimately they should be moving and looking at the same time but when coaching I believe focusing on movement first is the best way.

3. Decision-Did they make a clear and good decision? If they did, great! If they didn't, we have diagnosed a problem to which we must find a solution. A good question to use here would be "Tell me what you saw." The long term solution will obviously be continued coaching and exposure to decision making opportunities. Opportunity is the mother of improvement.

4. Execution- If a good decision is made, I will always support it. If it is not executed properly it is still a good decision. We simply need to improve the skill execution and this provides us with the context for which doing technical work is appropriate. The game has provided the 'need' and the 'why'.

A concept of passing I like to use with children is that; we pass "to" a teammate (or space)"not around" an opponent. You will often find that they will try to pass to a teammate when there is no clear pathway. In order words they are trying to pass 'around' the opposition. We are looking for a clear path to pass safely. Obviously as they begin to become more skilful they will begin to thread more delicate passes but to begin I think the concept of 'passing to' is very useful scaffolding. The receiver obviously plays a part in this and so we move to the concept of support.

Principles of Support (in possession)

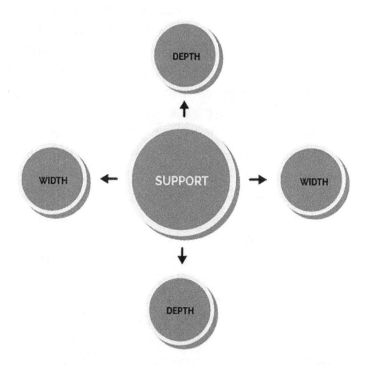

A player who can pass the ball accurately is of limited value unless they have potential receivers who have moved to support them or are attuned to the affordance. In order to do this, it is important that potential receivers are able to read the pattern of play. Movements made by players who do not have the ball (i.e. off-the-ball skills) are important and should be considered in games coaching. Help attune the players to the opportunities they can create for each other. Pattern recognition and understanding the principles of support play are key to this.

If your team has the ball you must support it intelligently. When coaching children, you must simplify the concept and provide them with multiple opportunities over time to figure it out for themselves. For me, the two most basic principles of supporting your teammate when they have the ball are; width and depth. The player on the ball will need support from either in front or behind (depth) or either side of them (width). In an ideal world, if all teammates are attuned to the player in possession needs, that player will have support from multiple directions and will therefore have multiple options. Raising awareness of the need for 'options' in possession is vital. This in turn will lead them to begin to be able to read the patterns of play.

As above; playing their role in providing a clear pathway so the person in possession can 'pass to' them is important to appreciate. Timing the support run is also an important concept. We want the receiver moving onto to the pass and taking it on the move. Providing these guidelines as well as prolonged exposure to these playing scenarios will assist the children in learning proper support play.

Principles of Defence and Attack- Space
If your team doesn't have the ball you must support them in getting it back. A full study of this whole area of support is too broad for the scope of this book. However, some simple concepts or principles may be of use to you.

One such concept or principle I use is "Space is time and time kills". This is true whether we are trying to create space for attacking or trying to limit space in order to defend. So the question for defenders will be "How can we minimise space for the opposition?" and for attackers it will be "How can we create space to attack?".

Coach the children the need to 'move in and out of space'. A concept I use is "There is no space if we simply stand in space. You must move in and out of space. It is the movement that creates the space and the problems for the defenders". In order for the team to learn to play together they must learn that they can make 'opportunities' for each other by getting 'out of space' and 'offering' it to their teammate to move into; collective or reciprocal action. Leaving space to move into as the play develops is another important concept.

When done appropriately, explaining the concept of perceiving 'shared affordances' to children is brilliant. It opens up a whole new world to them. It shows them the game is all about lines and angles, perceiving opportunities and creating problems for the opposition to solve. Team play is about inter- personal / inter- player synergies. 'Walk-throughs' are often useful for this but again keep it brief. Only use them when you sense the children are ready for them and interested in them. Done properly they will lead them to look at the game completely differently. We are changing perspective and raising awareness. We are bringing intelligence to the game and as intelligent beings they respond positively to it.

A concept or principle I use for defending is 'creating/ maintaining stability' and the opposite for attacking is 'creating instability/ breaking system stability'. So questions would be; how can we create and maintain stability in front of our goal? Alternatively, for attackers; how can we break system stability or create instability in front of the opposition's goal?

Principles of Tackling
When we understand these principles of defending the context is provided to work on the technical aspects of coaching the tackle at a higher level. The principles of tackling can largely be broken down into what is known as the 4D's; Delay, Deny Space, Dispossess, Develop Attack. Footwork and timing are critical components of tackling therefore physical literacy is key. For tackling; think- Feet! They will get them to where they need to be.

- Delay- Slow your opponent down; don't rush in.
- Deny Space- Get close and into their space.
- Disposes- When the opportunity presents itself make the tackle.
- Develop Attack;-In an ideal world you will have regained possession and so the focus turns to developing an attack.

So the Principles of the Game and appropriate use of concepts give you an excellent coaching resource. They can be used to diagnose, question and spot and raise awareness against the backdrop of the games based approach to coaching. Where appropriate, they are basically the narrative or cues of my in- game coaching.

Lifestyle

All great players are made at home, on the street, against the wall of the house, with their friends and so on. This is a well-recognised and established belief. A child can only develop their potential if they have sufficient exposure to the game and the skills of the game. The amount of exposure during games and formal practice doesn't suffice. The game needs time. That's why they need to practice at home.

Do you really want to be the coach who complains that the kids aren't practicing at home? Or do you want to be the coach who facilitates it, who actively and strategically promotes it? Can you see how this will pay rich dividends? Make it happen! Provide the incentive and the inspiration to make them want to learn and improve. Give the children some sort of Home Practice Notebook for the chosen sport or in some cases it could be merely daily exercise or activity, a Daily Practice Log. It can be simplest piece of paper or the fanciest glossiest document. In my club we call it 'My Hurling Home Practice Diary'.

Make a big deal about it. Check them weekly. Have a weekly raffle for those who bring them back each week. Promote and reward compliance and make it important. Always make learning and improvement important. Reward those who reach 'home practice targets'. Maybe have four numeric targets throughout the year and a prize for reaching each one, for example 20, 40, 60 and 100 practices. You could also do something like a 30-day home practice challenge. With this said, you must appreciate that this will only be a success if you set it up for success. The environment must be right. The respect and trust must be there. It must be managed properly.

The initial focus between say 5 and 9 years would be to imbed the culture of home practice. However, as the children mature, perhaps from 10 onwards, it may be appropriate that the focus can shift to the quality of that practice as they become mature enough to take ownership of their own improvement. In an ideal world we want what is termed 'deliberate practice'. There must be skill in the practice, skill in the repetition. Raise their awareness of this but make 'fun' the priority.

Deliberate Practice
Deliberate practice refers to a special type of practice that is purposeful and systematic. It requires focused attention and is conducted with the specific goal of improving performance. It differs from 'regular practice' in that regular practice might largely consist or mindless purposeless repetitions. Ecological Dynamics would underpin all high quality deliberate practice as it captures how learners effectively organise movement and build effective perception and action couplings.

The goal of deliberate practice is not to be enjoyed. Its only goal is to improve your performance. However, I feel this is not to say it cannot be enjoyed by those with the correct mindset. Satisfaction is to be gained through application and learning and this should be portrayed as fun. Deliberate practice requires sustained effort and concentration. It requires the learner to continuously challenge themself, set goals and practice at the edge of their ability. Its greatest challenge is to remain focused on improvement. The more we repeat a task the more mindless it can become. Mindless activity is the enemy of deliberate practice. Feedback is essential. Measurement is one means of feedback. What we measure we improve.

Jot down some ideas of how you can promote and inspire home practice among the children you coach.

_____

_____

Healthy Eating and Lifestyle

Promoting healthy eating and healthy life habits also comes in under this section. You obviously want your players eating well and resting well. Players with poor eating habits struggle with recovery and body composition issues as they get older. You must raise awareness of the importance of a healthy diet and lifestyle. If you have built a relationship of trust with the child through connection, they will value what you value and you will have the power to influence.

Alternatively, you could organise the visit of a professional in this area. Promote a healthy lifestyle and you will have healthier children on your team. Healthy children make healthy adults and healthy adults make good players.

What type of lifestyle do you want your players to have?

_____

_____

Summary Points

1. Appreciate the needs of the child.
2. Appreciate the developmental characteristics of the child.
3. Understand what motivates children and what leads them to contribute and give of their best.
4. Appreciate the learning process and the role mistakes play in it.
5. Foster and nurture a 'growth mindset' in the children you coach.
6. Commit to developing Physical Literacy in your children.
7. Understand the role of representative practice design in skill acquisition and work on improving your ability to create rich learning environments.
8. Learn the principles of the game you coach and use them as a means of coaching team play.
9. Facilitate and promote home practice among the children you coach.

Research is key!

Can you see?

CHAPTER 6
VALUES AND VISIONS

"This above all: to thine own self be true,
and it must follow, as the night the day,
Thou canst not then be false to any man"
Polonius - Hamlet, William Shakespeare

Your values will define you as a coach. Put simply your values are the most basic human message you wish to stand for. What do you see as important? Your values direct you towards what you feel is important. They allow you to know what you want to see. All too often we are not very good at understanding what it is that we really want. Our awareness is low.

Coaching is not about being perfect. If it was I would definitely be a non-runner. We really have to get away from this notion of perfection. In my opinion it really stifles us. It sends us in this self-preservation mode. We will all make mistakes and slip ups. We will say the wrong thing from time to time. However, building a strong values system into your coaching, and practicing it, will give you direction and build a strong culture within your team. Coach your values to create the culture. Be clear on what type of culture and environment you want to foster and build it with purpose and care. Environment is the guiding hand that shapes behaviour. The coach creates the environment and the culture; success follows. You must be willing to own this responsibility. The children will find important, what you purposefully make important. What do you value?

The REF Value System

For me when coaching children, it's always simply, 'Respect, Effort and Fun' (REF!). I reference them continuously against the children's' actions in my coaching. I drive them home. I can't make it any simpler, it encapsulates everything. For me it says to the children.

"Respect yourself, your teammates, your team and your coaches. Respect the facilities, equipment we use and our workspace. Respect the game we play. Respect our opposition and the referee. Always try your best. Have fun while playing and training."

I can often explore (not lecture) the various elements of REF with the group and get their input. Use a questioning style. *Give me one example you saw today of a teammate showing respect? Who do you think gave the best effort at training today?* Explore your values with the children and use them as a clear guide for them. Instil values in your team. They will be the fuel that drives everything.

Respect

Discipline is a scary word and denotes army major type connotations. There's a fine line between discipline and fun. It's the balance between maintaining stability and creating instability. Children must be free to express themselves. Respect is key.

"We work from a point of 'Respect' to a point of 'Connection'."

Connection within a group leads to success. Respect is the starting point. The journey starts there. It is most likely my number one value. We have nothing if we don't have a respectful team environment. All the knowledge in the world will be no good to you if you cannot create a culture of respect.

Discipline is simply respect. Coach respect, explore it with them, make it a thing not just a word. Raise awareness. Respect is actions not words. Only when there is true respect can there be enjoyment, fun and great coaching. I might refer to the word respect about five times in an hour session but I always reference it to some tangible act that has just occurred. When I see it, I endorse it (we will look at this shortly).

Respect involves treating children equally and giving them equal opportunity, equal challenge and equal assistance. Opportunity is the starting point of improvement. So if you are asking me should children get equal playing time no matter their ability the answer is? Yes! Especially so with 'younger kids'.

I would argue that perhaps as they move towards late childhood, say eleven or twelve years, it may be possible to introduce the concept of 'earning' equal playing time. To introduce this concept, the team environment must be healthy, the expectations extremely clear and the communication around it excellent. 'Earning' equal time may involve things such as honouring and being true to the team charter or team standards the children have had input in creating themselves or meeting home practice or training attendance targets. It is underpinned by the concept that they must earn the right to be treated equally. 'Earning' time has nothing to do with ability. Its principles are rooted in 'values'.

And so the environment created is based on a value for respect. It is the corner stone of great coaching. It works both ways. The coach respects the children and the children respect the coach. We work from a point of respect.

Effort
I consciously avoid placing any value on talent; instead I value 'effort' (we have seen this in Mindset and will see why again later). I want to produce courageous and honest sportspeople. I am coaching them to love to compete, to struggle, to embrace the challenge and persevere.

It is the learning player and team we want. A mantra I like to use in coaching is JEF, Judge Effort First. I think it's a great anchor for any coach. This value for 'effort' is what fuels application and engagement with the games based approach.

Fun

Fun is one of the main reasons children play sport, and lack of fun is one of the main reasons they give it up. The game needs time so if we can heighten their engagement with the game through making it fun it will have obvious positive knock on effects. There are multiple studies done in this area. Fun is simply another word for learning. Fun is so important in my coaching of children. I want them really enjoy coming training. I find being challenged appropriately brings a great sense of joy and fun to a child. They love to be stretched. They love to compete. This is fun for them.

A study undertaken in 2014 for George Washington University *(The fun integration theory: toward sustaining children and adolescents sport participation.)*, by researcher Amanda Visik interviewed numerous youth athletes and asked them why they played sports. 9 out of 10 said the number one reason they played was it was fun! They defined fun as; *trying their best, being treated respectfully by coaches, parents and teammates, and getting playing time.*

Great coaches are clear as to what they value and what they stand for. They stick to what they believe in and actively promote it among their players. They make their values the most important thing and if we make something the most important thing it is the most important thing. There is congruence in their values and actions. Values lived out are the underpinning strength and cultural driving force behind success.

What values do you want to instil in the children you coach?

_____

_____

What actions and behaviours do you think these values will drive among the children and the team?

_____

_____

A value-based motto could work for you in endorsing your values. Something you can repeat automatically and therefore keep it high on the team agenda. Examples of values based mottos are,

1. *"Show Respect, Give Your Best, Have Fun".*
2. *"Respect the Game, Respect Each Other, Play Hard".*

Come up with your own personal values based motto.

_____

_____

Visions

"An artist is not paid for his labour but for his vision."
James Whistler- American Artist

Your visions are your ultimate destinations. What would it look like in an ideal world? What are you aspiring towards and striving for? They drive awareness. Practicing proper coaching brings us to, or certainly towards, our destination but we must have a clear understanding of what it is we want to help create. I return the central quote of the book;

"I saw the angel in the marble and carved until I set him free."
Michelangelo-
Italian Sculptor, Painter and Architect
(on his sculpture of David)

Always start with the end in sight. Your vision should be your obsession. Where there is no vision there is little or no hope. They will inspire, inform and guide you and those in your care. Share them with your players. You are raising awareness. Create images in their head. Images lead to actions. A coach is always selling a vision. That is the job.

Below, I have gone through some of the areas for which I feel you must have a vision. I have added my own which are unique to me and may mean nothing to you. Create your own that are authentic and true to what you hope to achieve through your coaching. They may, and no doubt will, change and evolve over time.

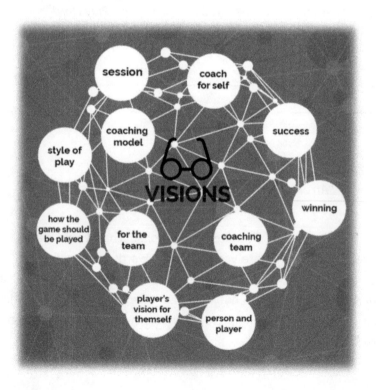

A Vision for Yourself as Coach

What type of coach do you want to be? What is your vision for yourself as coach? My Vision for myself as a child coach is 'Positively Different, Bringing Joy and Awareness'. It is unique to me and it means something to me. Perhaps something simpler and more tangible could be: Fun, Fair and Competent.

Write a vision for yourself as coach.

Curious, learning, growing

A Vision for Success

What will success look like for your coaching? For me, when dealing with children it's simply; smiling faces and a 'thank you'. I see success as a child genuinely thanking you after a session.

Success can be measurable for example player recruitment and retention. What is going to make this player keep coming back to your training sessions?

Whatever way you see success you must have a vision for it. Write a vision for success for your coaching.

A Vision for Winning

We can't talk about success without talking about winning. Traditionalists struggle with the fact that nowadays it seems popular to say child sport is not about winning and winning doesn't matter. I can see where they are coming from because they can't see a clear and tangible alternative.

Here I am talking about 'older children' from say 9 years upwards. I think winning is important, as is wanting to win and being self-driven to compete. No matter how you look at it team sport is about getting the better of your opponent through being the best you can be. Taking this away from a sport seems counterintuitive to me.

Children need to understand how it feels to lose. But they also have to see that it's not a devastating outcome. We want to coach children to learn how to compete and strive to overcome and win but in doing this we must be true to our values. This is why the value system is key. Being over- competitive can be a developmental killer and can bring out the worst in us as coaches.

Moving on from a more traditional view of winning, to a more tangible concept of what is all about, I think it make sense that, "It is about giving your best". This is why we value- Effort. My vision for winning is taken from a line in a poem;

> "Giving all, it seems to me, is not so far from victory."
> **The Road Ahead or the Road Behind- George Joseph Moriarty**

This is what I see as winning so even when we 'lose' we can 'win'. A motto of a team of U13's I am currently coaching is "Winning and losing is nothing; but to fight (in a sporting sense) is everything".

Coach them to compete. If we coach them to compete, winning will be the by-product. If we coach them to compete losing will be our teacher and will drive the desire to improve. Quite simply we are losing or we are learning. Coach through questioning- Did we fight? How can we compete better next time? Where do we need to improve? What did you learn?

> "Anger + Blame+ Complain = Defeat. Learning = Victory."

By helping children understand what is winning and what is losing, we are leading them to victory. Define winning for them. Provide them with a clear vision of it. Define losing for them. Winning is not bad and wanting to win isn't bad however; there are deeper more tangible qualities we can develop and focus on. Focus on what is needed to win and winning will just happen.

From a pure coaching perspective, you are obviously far wiser to focus all your attention on the results of your coaching instead of focusing only on the winning and losing. Easier said than done sometimes, I know.

Finally, never confuse winning with performance and be sure to coach your children the same. Often the most dangerous moment comes with victory. You don't have to play well to win or badly to lose. Performance is something different than the result. The race is long but in the end it's only with ourselves.

What does winning and losing mean to you? What is your vision for winning?

_____

_____

To what degree do you allow the scoreboard and the game's outcomes determine, influence or effect how you coach children?

_____

_____

A Vision for your Coaching Team

What type of a coaching team do you want to be part of? A team can be defined as having,

"A number of people with complementary skills who are committed to a common purpose, performance goals, and a common approach for which they hold themselves mutually accountable."

Such a broad skill set is required to share the workload around to provide the optimal learning environment. As coach you should be recruiting good people to perform tasks that are relative to their skill set. The more, good people you can get and the more you can get these good people contributing the better.

For me the vision for the coaching team is:

- Connected, Contributing, Caring and Competent- CCCC

Write a vision for your coaching team.

_____

_____

How can you help to ensure this vision becomes a reality?

_____

_____

A Vision for the Person and the Player

What are the sporting and non-sporting qualities you want in your player? The non-sporting qualities are just as important and the sporting qualities. These are the qualities that will make them a good team mate and allow them make the best of their sporting abilities and qualities. These non-sporting qualities must be given due consideration and fostered and nurtured from the very beginning. It is the best, if not the only time to do this. You are embedding these qualities into the very core of the player. You are raising awareness of what is needed to succeed.

My vision for the person is that they are honest and of good character, independent, self-reliant and self-aware. I want them to be 'problem solvers' not 'giver outers'. I want them to be 'team first' and place service ahead of self. I want them to be 'excellent learners'. More so than anything else; sport is a learning competition. I purposely work to 'draw out' these qualities in the child. We are always working purposefully towards the future.

What is your vision for the person?

_____

_____

With regard to the player, I want them to be totally adaptable to whatever happens in front of them.

"A completely adaptable and efficient player; physically, technically, tactically and mentally. Any ball, any challenge, any option, anyway, any day. They can play the game or perform the skill whatever way is best in that moment. A ferocious competitor"

They are like water. Water is image I use for my vision of the player.

"Empty your mind...be shapeless, formless...like water. When you pour water in a cup, it becomes the cup. When you pour water in a bottle, it becomes the bottle. When you pour water in a teapot, it becomes the teapot. Water can drip and it can crash. Become like water my friend."
Bruce Lee- Martial Artist

I design practices with a view to helping create this vision.

Write a vision for your player.

_____

_____

A Player's Vision for Themselves

Remember; raise awareness, awaken the player. Organise a suitable, off-field, sit down exercise to facilitate this. Explain the different elements or pillars of a player to them: Mental, Physical, Technical/

Skill, Tactical/ Team Play and Lifestyle, and let them build their vision of themselves.

Referencing a player, they admire is always a good idea. A child of nine or ten years will be able to do this if you explain it to them properly. Lead them to understand that they are the masters of their own destinies. Awareness is the first step of the journey.

A Vision for the Team

What is your vision for your team? For me it's simple; Unified, Strong and Adaptable - USA. I design my practice to unite the team, make them strong in every pillar and trust that they will grow to be adaptable.

Write a vision for your team. Again, a suitable exercise can be used to get the players input into this.

_____

_____

A Vision for how the Game should be Played
How do you believe the game should be played? Personally I believe the game should be played with joy. The secret to joy is freedom and the secret to freedom is courage.

What is your vision for the way the game should be played?

_____

_____

A Vision for the Style of Play

This begins to become important when dealing with children from about ten years onwards. What style of play you would like your players to play should have a direct influence on the content of your training session design. Ask yourself; what do you want the team to do?

- When we have the ball…

_____

- When we don't have the ball…

_____

You can also possible consider; what do we do…

- When we lose the ball…

_____

- When we win the ball

_____

Build the playing style around these concepts. Keep it simple. Don't confuse variety for sophistication. Simplicity is the ultimate form of sophistication.

A Vision for your Coaching Model

This is more so for the club, which we will look at shortly. It is almost like an overview of how you do things. If someone flew over your club in the morning and all the child teams were training, what would the overriding observations be? For me the vision would be; 'All children are active. The Coach facilitates. The children are learning through games and by playing the game itself. People are smiling'.

Write a vision for your Coaching Model.

_____

_____

A Vision for your Session

Session Planning

At this stage in the book you have covered a great deal of what is necessary to coach successfully. If you have completed the exercises you have a clear vision of what you want your coaching world to look like. If you haven't completed the exercises thus far in the book I suggest you go back and do so now or else commit to doing so sometime in the near future. My aim here is to challenge you to design practices that are true to who you are as a coach.

Through reading the book you have completed enough research to know what is good for the child and should be in a position to meet them where they are at with the appropriate challenge and assistance. You know your KCPs and Coaching Cues, Principles of the Game and that games are a superior way to coach. You are aware that guided discovery and questioning are excellent coaching methodologies. You understand you are merely raising awareness. You have a clear vision of what it is you are trying to achieve. Everything until this point must now feed into your session. Coaching is practice not theory so now you must put everything into practice.

Plans are nothing but planning is everything. Precision in planning will lead to precision in performance. I really must drive this message home. Planning is absolute key. You are not planning for the sake of planning you are planning in order to improve as a coach. Your session plan is your vision for the session: how it should look ideally. If you don't plan it the chances are you won't do it. All sessions must have purpose, competition and game speed.

Obviously, as an amateur coach your planning time is limited and cannot take up an inordinate amount of time but I really must urge you to invest in your planning. Session planning is the only way I can see in which you can gain significant traction in coaching improvement. You will become more efficient the more you practice it and begin to refine and get a feel for what's important. Throughout your coaching career you should invest blocks of time in planning and at other stages it might not be as important.

Write out your plan and bring it with you on a clipboard. Hold the clipboard in your hand throughout the session and so you can reference it. Bring a pencil too. Do all your thinking before the session and your coaching during it. Plan your work, and then work your plan. On occasion the balance between sticking to the plan and being a slave or fool to it can be a difficult one to navigate. Without doubt, we need a degree of flexibility in our session delivery and practice design to address emerging information and situations. This allows us to address what is happening in front of us in the moment. However, my advice is that, to begin with, for the majority of the time you should stick to your plan. In this way if you notice something in the session like for example a lack of skill required to do complete a task properly, or if something comes into your head, you can jot it down in session and add it to your plan for the following session. If you invest time in your planning, within reason, you should invest the time in executing it.

Time is Precious

Have a stop watch (not a phone) and time everything. Plan the timing of the activities and stick to the timings. It provides clarity to the challenge for the children. If you think the time was too short jot it down on your plan, there and then and use this information when planning your next session. You are reflecting and learning in session. The process is learning.

Time the transitions between sections of the session. Managing transitions from one game or activity to another is vital. An inordinate amount of time can be lost here. Set a time limit on transitions for the children and for yourself. Set a time limit on water breaks. If you give them forever they will take forever; if you give them 45 seconds, they will move quickly (SAID Principle).

I always want what I call "density" in the session. Timing things helps me pack in lots of elements into the session. There is little or no down time. If the session is well connected and flows, we can stay learning.

Sometimes the stopwatch isn't king. When asking questions, allow them the time to answer, you will have this allowed for in your plan but you don't have to stick rigidly to it. The more time you give them the more efficient they will become in answering. Factor questioning time into your session but; be fluid.

Below I will give you some ideas around planning but I really want you to personalise your planning. Make your work and then make your work, work for you. Set yourself up for success. Here are some suggested content/categories for your session plan/vision. Do you need to use all of them? No is the answer, but using the majority of them over time will give you a deep understanding of what you are trying to achieve and how you can achieve it.

"Personalise your Planning"

Your planning will evolve over time as you learn what works best for you. You are planning in order to learn your craft; what works for you and the children and what doesn't? You are using planning in order to deliver and refine your 'Coaching World'.

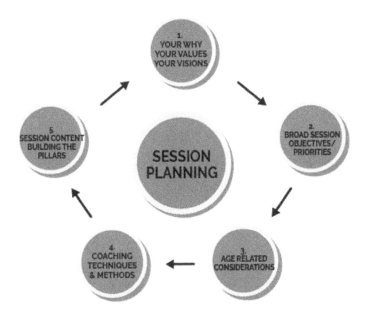

Your Why, Your Values & Your Visions
Always keep them in front of you. They must be to the forefront in everything you do.

- Why do you coach children
- Your Values/Team Values
- Vision for yourself as coach/your coaching team
- Vision for your players
- Vision for your team
- A Vision for success
- A Vision for how the game should be played

Broad Session Objectives/ Session Priorities.
These are broad objectives you want to achieve and will be directly related to your values and visions. Being truthful, they often remain the same from session to session and are a rundown of many of the elements of the Carver. Examples of the broad session objectives are,

- Connect with every player.
- Players have fun, learn respect for coaches and teammates, group is socialised.
- Promote and endorse your values. Respect, Effort and Fun.
- All pillars of the player are addressed; Mental, Physical, Technical/ Skill, Tactical/ Team Play.
- Improve our use of the ball when we have it.

Age Related Considerations- Who is in front of you?

This is important in order for you to have an appreciation of what the child should be doing. For example;

- In a session for7 year old boys a broad focus should be on developing FMS and sports postures.
- In a session for 11-year-old boys the 'window of accelerated adaptation to motor coordination' (i.e. the skills of the game) must be considered. All FMS should be further developed and general overall sports specific skills should be learnt during this phase.

Coaching Techniques and Methodologies
- Constraint Led/ Games Based Approach.
- Endorsing (See next).
- Spot and raise awareness.
- Coach by Contrast- Give them options A or B.
- Coach by Questioning- Have your questions prepared.
- Coach directly when needed and cue the KCP's.
- Facilitate 'Player to Player' Coaching.

Session Content- Building The Pillars.

How are you going to build the pillars of the player? The session must have the appropriate physical, technical/ skill, tactical/ team play and mental challenges. All the pillars must be purposefully built in every session (perhaps less so the tactical with very young children but keep it in mind).

Design physical, technical/ skill and tactical/ team play games and challenges. Your values will look at the mental side, so for me, it's respect and effort and these are constantly reinforced.

Subcategories within Session Content.

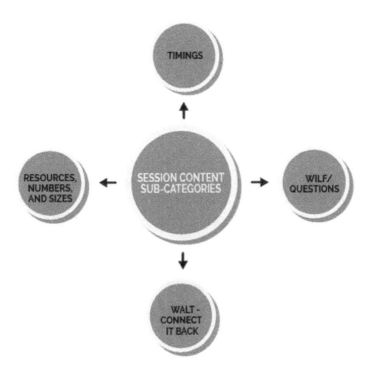

- **Timings-**How long are you going to spend at each section? How long are you going to allow to transition from one exercise to the next?
- **WILF-** WILF stands for: What I'm looking for. You must know exactly what you're looking for in each exercise or game in the session. This will help you to endorse it which we will see shortly, e.g. nice change of direction/ vision etc.
- **KCPs and Coaching Cues-** What are the KCP's of the skills and cues for coaching them?

- **Questions-** Prepare appropriate questions for games and activities- Think; What, Why, When, How, Where and Who.

- **WALT** stands for "We are learning to". Use this concept to help raise the children's awareness of what they are learning to do and why they are learning to do it. Connect everything to the game and the principles and concepts of the game and show them where it fits in. At the start of each section you can explain what they are learning to do and where it fits in to performance in the game. Your WALT is your, and indeed their, "Why". They need to know; why.

- **Resources, Numbers and Sizes-** Know what equipment you will need. Know or estimate what numbers you will be catering for. Know the sizes of the play zone or pitches that will be appropriate to cater for the numbers you have. This can be trial and error but document it during the session e.g. "pitch too small for 4 v 4 at 25m x 20m, make bigger for next session."

(See appendix for example of a session plan and a model session plan template)

Now you have a 'Vision for the Session' and so you have a great chance of making that vision a reality. I assume at this point that you are somewhat overwhelmed and asking yourself, how can I do all of this?

A System that leads to a Style

For me, learning to coach can be likened to learning to cook. In cooking at first it is a good idea to religiously follow a recipe. The recipe gives you a framework to begin cooking in a structured manner. Eventually, as you develop your craft, you understand what the reasons for the different ingredients are. Then you can start to mix, match, experiment, refine and put you own twist on it based on the knowledge you've attained by practicing cooking. The process has made you a better cook and fluidity comes to your cooking style.

Similarly, I believe developing or adopting a systematic approach to how you coach your plan is a great starting point for you. You may need a system to execute your plan; a plan to deliver the plan. Following a system will lead you to developing a style or your 'own way'.

Children respond excellently to clarity and consistency. In the appendix I have included two systems you may find useful to use or adapt.

- The first system can be used and modified to coach any Sports Specific Skills or FMS in a play zone (as referenced in Chapter 5).
- The second system is very much suited to the FMS games *(see appendix).*

The systems are very similar (virtually the same, to be honest) but for clarity I have separated them. They are extremely simple. The rationale behind the systems is that they are a means to facilitating a dialogical, consistent and supportive environment. They are a step by step approach which facilitates all the elements of Carver and your Session Plan/Vision. When starting with a new group of children I will stick quite rigidly to the system. As their 'coachability' improves over time through use of the system, the need for slavish adherence to the steps is lessened; however, I never deviate too far. As you use it will become more of a coaching style rather than you following a system. Play with it, adapt it and use it to develop your own style of coaching.

I must also note again that you must continuously work on keeping your talking or instruction brief. Aim for under 30 seconds at a time. Anything over it is a lecture and lectures should be kept to a minimum. Use your stopwatch. Hold yourself accountable. We are pushing for experiential learning.

(See appendix for Coaching System.)

Discipline

It must be noted that coaching is not a fairytale and we will always meet challenging behaviour when dealing with children. What is important is that we deal with it in a fair, consistent and transparent manner. Below is a rundown of how you can approach challenging behaviour. It is a good idea to explain this consistently to the children and of course to the parents.

The ethos towards 'in-session discipline' should one of positive reinforcement whereby we continually promote our values (REF) and seek to elicit, encourage and endorse the desired behaviours. We want children to understand and appreciate the power of REF. We must appreciate that all children are different and we cannot expect children to be perfect; however, through use of a disciplinary system you are giving them a great opportunity to conform.

When and if the need arises, you should employ a structured and fair disciplinary system which is clearly explained to the children. The child will initially get a 'verbal reasoning' using the language of REF, e.g. "You are not respecting the game/your team mate. You know that is what we do here and you know that is what is expected of you." If the behaviour continues the child will be asked to "sit out" for two minutes. Should this not resolve the situation, the child's behaviour should be discussed directly with the parent.

Conflict Resolution among Children

'Rock, Paper, Scissors' can to be used to resolve any conflict within a game or exercise. It is an amazingly simple and useful tool. Teach it to the children and encourage its use. It works a treat.

Summary Points

1. Know what you value and endeavour and plan to be true to this.
2. Start with the end in sight. Come up with your visions and work towards them.

3. Use your values and visions as the starting point when planning your sessions.
4. Plan your work, work your plan.
5. In order to develop a style of coaching it may be a good idea to follow a systematic approach to begin with.

Values and Visions are key!

Can you see?

CHAPTER 7
ENDORSING

I urge you to really focus on this area. This is vital in coaching children. If mastered, it will virtually eliminate frustration and negativity in your coaching. Develop your 'Endorsement Lens'. It will be one of your greatest tools.

Every day I deal with children the power of what I call 'endorsing' impresses me. As coach it is a difficult one to conquer because it is dependent on your knowledge and capacity in the previous four elements of the Carver Model. To endorse effectively you must be able to assess and observe properly. If you clearly know what to look for you will be able to see it. This will allow you to;

"Shine a light on what is right."

Endorsing is simply acknowledging something you have noticed that's already there; an observation you share, about positive things in a child's performance, ability, attitude or behaviour. It is being a 'noticer', an 'encourager'. Endorsing is a positive means of getting your message across and has its roots in the quickly expanding field of Positive Psychology. It is to be dovetailed with what we have learned about raising awareness.

It is my belief that no coach intentionally sets out to be negative. For me, it's just they don't possess the skills to be positive. Positivity is a buzzword nowadays and this is obviously positive! However, the positivity that is pedalled commercially can be something of a vague and hollow concept. Everything seems to be 'amazing', 'awesome' or some other superlative. In truth, it is artificial positivity.

Awareness of negativity is great but simply trying to be more positive is a really hard concept to encapsulate and master. Endorsing is specific praise. It is seeing and affirming. It is not vague, hollow or patronising. You must move away from the 'Good Boy/ Girl' type tokenism and get into specifically endorsing the behaviours or processes you want. It is precision in praise.

"Precision in praise"

Proper research, will lead you to understanding child development and learning, physical literacy, skill acquisition, the principles and concepts of the game, your 'Values' and 'Visions' and will lead you to understand what it is you want to see in the children you coach. Your planning and 'Vision for your Session' will ensure all the thinking has been done before the session and to begin you may have a systematic approach to how you're going to run the session. All the hard work is done. You know what you are looking for (WILF). In coaching children, if you look hard enough you will always find what you're looking for. Vision trumps all other senses. Visual processing doesn't just assist in the perception of what's unfolding in front of you. It dominates it.

Knowing what you actually want will enable you to endorse it when you see it. It will allow you to be 'positive'. The more you endorse the more you see or, the more accurately, the more the children 'do'.

The best way I can explain this is through my understanding of the Reticular Activation System in your brain. Put simply there is a network of nerves in your brain that control your state of awareness and attention. This system functions as a filter to accept and reject the overwhelming amount of stimuli that we all encounter when we are awake. You can actively set this 'filter' by choosing to think about certain things, or it will be set by the environment.

RAS
ALLOWS YOU TO FOCUS ON WHAT YOU VALUE.
SUPPORTS YOU WHEN YOU SET GOALS.

One of the most familiar examples is when a person buys a new car. It seems that when you have that new car that many cars just like it suddenly appear everywhere you go! They were really there all the time you just noticed them now. Why is that? It is because you have set your 'RAS' to look for that model of car. Another example of this is if you are building a house. I remember trying to choose a design for the front wall of my house and all of a sudden I began to notice walls I had driven past all my life and only now was I 'seeing' them. When we choose to set our RAS, we set the direction of our behaviour.

Through setting the RAS on what it is you want to see in the children it is amazing how powerful it can be for your coaching. Now, don't get too carried away, it is that simple but not that easy. You really need to know your stuff here. You need to have your research and planning done otherwise it will be just hollow tokenism. Everything needs to be spot on; carefully worded. If all is in order the dialogue of the session may be a more natural and organic version of something like.

"Lovely small steps from Damien to avoid contact" "Nice Gary ...you moved immediately when you got the ball" "Good decision to shoot, Barry" "Look at Anthony, listening very closely to me" "Great sportsmanship there from Darragh; accepting the referee's decision" "Excellent bravery from Cathal." "Excellent support running from George... moving into the space."

"Praise the act not the child."

Jot down some examples of how you would like the narrative of your session to sound.

_____

_____

I am being really honest here in saying that if delivered correctly this approach will spread the desired actions and behaviours through your players. Children aim to please. Simply asking the question, *"Who's listening quietly there? Oh Brian. Great! Thank you Brian"* will have the vast majority quiet in no time if you acknowledge them one by one as they begin to conform. *"Thanks TJ, thanks Declan, lovely Stephen, oh great and a smile as well from Sean. "*You are simply fulfilling the needs of the children, which are to be recognised and praised.

Now I understand many of you are reading this and thinking this all sounds great in theory but there is a need for a bit of directness. I totally agree! It is not all sweetness and light. Our job is to challenge and assist. We must challenge. We must stretch. As children get older and indeed as you get to know them better, you can be more direct, demanding and challenging. In fact, your ability to endorse will make your more direct and challenging approach all the more powerful. The relationship you have developed with them, that 'connection', will allow you challenge them when they aren't living up to all they can be. There are frequently times when we must simple call the behaviour what it is. We don't want to contribute to 'praise addiction', neediness or 'learned helplessness'. It is ok to be demanding. Accountability is good. I am proud to consider myself a demanding coach.

"If you treat an individual as he is, he will remain how he is. But if you treat him as if he were what he ought to be and could be, he will become what he ought to be and could be."
Johann Wolfgang von Goethe- German Writer

Please don't get bogged down in perfection here; as a Coach your goal is always improvement not perfection. Be advised that it will take you about five training sessions with the children to have this endorsement model fully up and running. You will have to directly teach them, or raise their awareness, of a number of values, visions, principles and concepts in the first few weeks. You can get endorsing straight away but your endorsements will become really powerful when the proper foundation is laid.

Support for the concept of 'endorsing' can be gained from the work of Carol Dweck on Mindset which we have referenced in Chapter 5. We "Endorse" our "Values" and our "Visions". We always "Value" effort not talent.

"Judge Effort First"- JEF

Below I have again adapted the text from *The Scientific American Special Editions Volume 23, Issue 55* .

The Secret to Raising Smart Kids-

In studies involving several hundred fifth graders published in 1998, for example, psychologist Claudia M. Mueller, now at Stanford, and I gave children questions from a nonverbal IQ test. After the first 10 problems, on which most children did fairly well, we praised them.... for their intelligence: "Wow...that's a really good score. You must be smart at this." We commended others for their process: "Wow...that's a really good score. You must have worked really hard. "We found that intelligence praise encouraged a fixed mind-set more often than did pats on the back for effort. Those congratulated for their intelligence, for example, shied away from a challenging assignment—they wanted an easy one instead—far more often than the kids applauded for their process. (Most of those lauded for their hard work wanted the difficult problem set from which they would learn.) When we gave everyone hard problems anyway, those praised for being smart became discouraged, doubting their ability. And their scores, even on an easier problem set we gave them afterward, declined as compared with their previous results on equivalent problems. In contrast, students praised for their hard work did not lose confidence when faced with the harder questions, and their performance improved markedly on the easier problems that followed.

Our work shows that praising a child's intelligence makes a child fragile and defensive. So, too, does generic praise that suggests a stable trait, such as "You are a good artist." Praise can be very valuable, however, if it is carefully worded. Praise for the specific process a child used to accomplish something fosters motivation and confidence by focusing children on the actions that lead to success. Such process praise may involve commending effort, strategies, focus, persistence in the face of difficulty, and willingness to take on challenges.

Again 'endorsing' is about supporting the process and being precise in our praise. List what you see as the advantages of using the concept of 'endorsing 'in your coaching?

_____

_____

Endorsing Home Practice

We want to create a culture of and respect for home practice; we want to support it and support those who embrace it. Please see Lifestyle section in Chapter 5.

Catchphrases, Maxims and Life Lessons

This chapter would not be complete for me without mentioning the use of catchphrases, maxims and life lessons in coaching. They are an excellent way to encapsulate your message and ensure that you;

"Keep the most important thing the most important thing."

They allow you to continuously drive home your most important messages in a concise manner. You are automating the message and driving it home unconsciously; you are automating your endorsement. You are continuously bringing to the forefront what you feel is most important. By using them repeatedly the message is clear and consistent. Here are some of my favourites.

"In unity there is strength."

"Winning and losing is nothing but to fight is everything."

"Set yourself up for success."

"Never let what you can't do get in the way of what you can do."

"The Give to Get Scale. You must give in order to get."

"Precision is how you win."

"WIN- What's Important Now?"

"First Mistake- Second Mistake!
The first mistake is ok; the second mistake is not."

"If it is to be, it's up to me."

"We're learning- Always learning!"

"Figure it out- Find a Way- Be Water. "

"Maximise Possession!"

"Everything follows effort- Perfect effort!"

"If one pass will do don't use two."

"It doesn't make you a bad person."

Endorsement is a powerful concept and tool in coaching. It heightens the coach's awareness of the child's positive actions every time they see them and as a consequence they see them often. It gets the coaches away from focusing on the outcome and instead focuses their attention to the processes involved in the outcome e.g. "I love the way you used little steps to avoid contact" (in the run up to the goal) instead of "great goal". The coach endorses the action and not the outcome because they understand that over time if they continue to do the right things the outcomes will take care of themselves. Endorse what you do want to see as opposed to wrestling with what you don't want.

"Specific Endorsement will lead to specific adaptation. SAID Principle"
(kind of!)

Summary Points
1. If you know what you're looking for it can be easy to see it.
2. Be specific with your feedback and weight it heavily in the affirming category.

Endorsing is key!

Can you see?

CHAPTER 8
REFLECTION

> *"We do not learn from experience...*
> *we learn from reflecting on experience."*
> John Dewey-
> American Philosopher, Psychologist, and Educational Reformer

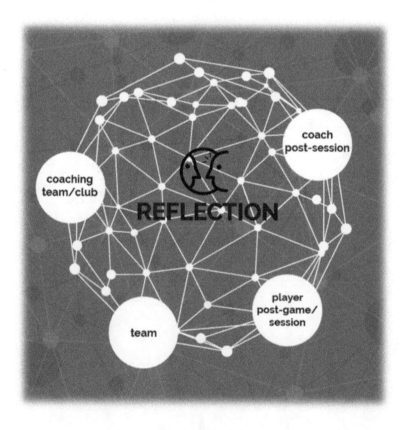

Coach Reflection Post Session

The session is now complete. How did it go? How was your delivery? What did you learn? What's important now ("WIN"). Coaching is about learning, improving and refining; developing your craft. Awareness will lead you to reflect and in turn reflection will drive your awareness. It is a cycle.

Reflection is an ongoing personal process and can be done in many manners and forms. Beginning out in your coaching career I believe it is vital to prioritise reflection and I feel if you practice it with discipline you will learn its value and refine and improve the practise of it as you go along. A common theme across all the research and literature in coaching is of the coach as a reflective learner. Reflection allows for steady, incremental, consistent improvement and drives accountability.

It is one thing to have built your 'coaching world' through research and to set out your values and visions and plan and work your session. However, what is truly important is that you constantly hold yourself accountable to honouring your 'coaching world'. Having the discipline to drive self-accountability is critical. Your effectiveness as a coach will be determined by your ability to continually plan, practice, reflect and refine. Evaluated experience is the best teacher.

A simple, tick the box reflection log can work wonders here. Other methods work well too. Humans have a great capacity for self-deception but an exercise like this can help you assess where you are. Reflection is a process of self-discovery. As we are discovering ourselves we are creating ourselves.

I firmly believe you should actively reflect after each session. Indeed, as I have mentioned in the planning section, I believe you can reflect in-session by jotting down observations on the session plan e.g. "grid too big, not enough time here, players didn't understand", etc. After the session you should then reflect some more on the session plan itself, and the players' response to it, jotting down simple notes on the content of the session and what the players need more of etc. Ask yourself "what's important now?" (WIN). This type of reflection is basically a needs analysis. Use this feedback to feed forward into you next session plan. Connect one session to another. Remember the key role of 'connection' in coaching.

Next I suggest you complete another reflection exercise on your delivery of the plan, i.e. how you coached the plan. All this information will lead into the planning of your next session. It is a cyclical process and a critical one if improvement in coaching is the goal. The law of consistency is key here.

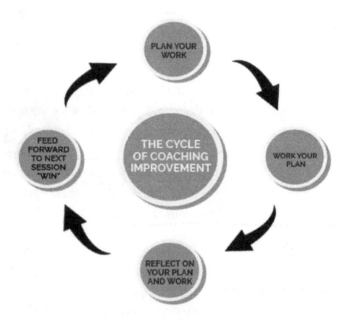

Without reflection you will really never learn what works for you. We never refine, simplify or evaluate. You will try something new for a period and forget about it when the next new thing comes along. You will flicker aimlessly from session to session, year to year and gain no traction in your coaching. Your learning will be sporadic. You will end up having variety for the sake of variety. Remember variety in coaching sessions isn't necessarily a good thing. You must know why you are doing what you are doing.

Reflection can be as basic or as complex as you want to be. It can be as simple sitting down and thinking; what worked well? What didn't work so well and how can I change it? What do the children need next? What do I need to do more of? What can I do less of? How can I do this better?

Reflection can be tedious and so it is important to streamline it and make it time efficient and focused. It is important to give it focus and structure, thereby making it more accurate and efficient. In the appendix I have provided a sample of a post training session 'Coach Reflection Log' you can copy or adapt. It is basic but it holds you accountable at many level. Ten areas scored from 1 to 10; giving you a percentage score. Be honest with yourself. Every session will not be excellent or indeed very good. If you are a creative coach often you will be pushing the boundaries in session design and as a result, things won't work out as planned. This is perfectly fine. On average I score between 60 and 70% on my own session reflection. The categories which I rate myself often change depending on what the team needs.

"Coaching is not about self-preservation it's about self-improvement."

Remember coaching is a craft you must nurture and develop. Many and most of the answers to coaching lie within. The challenge is to access these solutions. Reflection is key.

List some of the advantages of reflecting on your coaching.

_____

_____

(See appendix for Coach Reflection Log)

Player's Reflection Log

From time to time you can try a player reflection log. Obviously it needs to be age appropriate but I contend that the average child of ten years and above is well able for it. Raise their awareness of the value of reflection. Just as you learn to coach, they can learn to play. Developing the skills of self-regulated learning behaviours is vital. Developing this self-awareness, self-reliance and self-actualisation will have positive transfer to the child's life beyond sport. You are educating them to take responsibility for their own development and improvement.

Often we underestimate children. The content of some of the academic work they are doing in school would amaze you. They are continuously reflecting on their work at school as part of a new approach to personalising their learning in academia. Why not reflect on their learning in sport? The purpose of an exercise like this is to raise awareness of areas they are strong in and areas they may need to work on; one of the principles of deliberate practice. It gives them ownership of their own improvement in the sport and provides focus, direction and autonomy. Bring them to a quiet room after a match and let them complete the exercise. Alternatively, let them bring them home. They might not all return them but again you can incentivise this. Make it important!

Managed properly the player reflection log is a lovely exercise. Obviously if it is over- used it will become tedious and ineffective. Maybe three times over the course of a season would be good. As with everything we do the team culture and environment will determine its effectiveness.

Player reflection raises their awareness of what is important in order to perform and their own personal role in self-improvement. It facilitates self- actualisation. They learn that;

"If it is to be, it's up to me"

(See appendix for Player Reflection Log)

You could also try something like this after a training session, a five-minute exercise to reflect on their application to the session. You are merely raising awareness or drawing attention to...

What are the benefits of facilitating player reflection?

_____

_____

Team Reflection

The team belongs to the players so the same follows that every so often we should reflect as a team and ensure we are moving in the direction we wish. The Team Charter (see Chapter 3) will be the reference point here and this charter will be updated and reviewed as part of the team reflection process.

Coaching Team/Club Reflection

The very same holds true for the coaching team and club. The club must schedule repeated cycles of reflection and assessment. Plan, Do and Reflect. It is a never ending cycle of improvement and accountability. These reflection exercises must be facilitated in a professional manner. As with most things it's not simply what we do, it's how we do it.

Summary Points
1. Individually and collectively we learn from reflecting on our experiences.
2. A systematic approach to reflection can be an excellent way to promote ongoing improvement and learning.

Reflection is key!

Can you see?

CHAPTER 9
COHESIVE COLLECTIVE COACHING
AND THE CLUB COACHING MODEL

"We are many, but are we much?"
John Wooden- Legendary Basketball Coach

A Sporting Club or organisation is a living breathing entity. It can be in good health or poor health. A healthy club or sporting organisation can be characterised as one which is constantly strengthening its capacity as a place in which to play, coach and develop. Motivation is driven by the culture of a club, and that culture is created by its management and coaches. Culture drives expectations & beliefs, which in turn drive behaviours. I believe it is the club's responsibility to actively and continually recruit, develop and up skill it's coaches. It is this process that creates the culture. Coach education is key in any club. The Club should and must be a 'learning organisation'.

As we have seen, a team can be defined as having a number of people with complementary skills who are committed to a common purpose, performance goals, and a common approach for which they hold themselves mutually accountable. It is only logical that clubs should strive to create a 'cohesive coaching structure' within their club.

I have been fortunate to have worked with a number of progressive clubs to assist them in developing youth/child coaching and coaching structures in their club. I am also on that same journey in my own club. It is a never ending. The struggle is the pathway. Perseverance is crucial.

The aim is to create player and coach pathways. I believe it may be necessary for many amateur child or teen clubs to enlist the services of a coaching consultant. I honestly believe the right person can have a profound effect on coaching in the club. This professional can help drive and facilitate the coaching and club reflection process. Can this be done in-club by an in- club volunteer? Of course it can, provided the volunteer has the appropriate skills, time and motivation.

Every club needs their own unique and authentic Child and Youth Club Coaching Manual. This document should be created through a process of facilitated meetings with all coaches and members input. It must be an authentic document created by the club and should act as a template which empowers the club and its coaches to develop; the chosen sport, physical literacy, health and respect among its youth and foster a healthy sporting culture for its members. It must also be a living, breathing, evolving document.

In short, it should provide a collective vision for the club; a comprehensive, standardised and cohesive coaching plan based on best practices and principles. Consider the following…

Does it make sense that;

- Coach A comes in one year, without any real or meaningful training, guidance or up skilling and does and expects x, y and z from the kids. Their version of the game.
- Coach B comes in the following year, again with little training and does and expects completely different things. Their version of the game.
- Coach C follows the next year with his/her version and so on and so on.

Indeed, Coach A, B and C could all be coaching in the same coaching team at the same time. I'm sure you can appreciate that this is far from optimal?

List some of the consequences of lack of coaching alignment.

_____

_____

Cohesive Collective Coaching- The Club Coaching Model
Where appropriate I feel, a Coaching Model which aims to ensure each session exposes the children to FMS and a Games Based Approach to skill acquisition, is an idea worth exploring. This model can be circuit like (as below), with the children divided into small groups of maybe six or eight and rotated through the stations approximately every ten or fifteen minutes. This model requires large numbers of coaches but also provides an opportunity to recruit and develop coaches. New and improving coaches can work their way through the various stations over the course of the season and gain experience in coaching FMS, Games and Skills. Everyone has a part to play and everyone is needed.

In my opinion, a club should be constantly welcoming a wide range of Key Opinion Leaders into their club to give coach education workshops on a broad range of topics. It helps creating and sustain a culture of learning among coaches and provides the appropriate infrastructure and support.

In a club, especially at child and youth level, no coach can work in isolation. I believe in the power of Cohesive Collective Coaching. The power of the collective is probably the one thing that attracts me most to sport and coaching. 'In Unity there is Strength' is a message I continually deliver in the team sport environment. It is amazing what can be accomplished when people work together.

"In Unity there is Strength."

In a Cohesive Collective Coaching Model there should be a relatively standardised coaching approach and methodology, a common set of values, expectations, a consistent environment, a vision for their players, a vision for their coaches etc. The coaches work together towards these common visions and have the humility to ignore perceived individual accomplishments, instead contributing to the collective objectives. In order for this alignment to occur the conditions have to be right. The Club Coaching Manual must be a living, breathing, evolving document which is continually referenced, improved and updated. Whole club reflection must be practiced. It is a cyclical process.

There is no need to expand further, just to say, imagine if the child from the age of 6 to 18 (and into adulthood) received the same messages,

"Show respect, try your best, practice at home, compete hard, learn from mistakes, make friends, win or lose always look to learn and come back better and stronger. Be the best you can be."

Imagine the scope for self-improvement afforded to child and coach within this consistently healthy sporting environment. Imagine if they were continually met with the appropriate challenges and assistance. Can you see the scope of Cohesive Collective Coaching? Imagine how strong the club would be and how sustainable the model would be. Coaches and players would be free to come and go but the culture would remain the same; a complete support network for learning.

"No experts. No guru's. Just learners!"

A Team Administration Person is one vital role you must recruit. This person takes care of all the logistics of the team; the text messaging, the first aid, managing the Home Practice Model (if you have it); basically everything except the coaching of the team. They are really the 'Mother Hen' or 'Godfather' type figure of the team, and it is a role many people enjoy.

I must caution that real and meaningful change takes time, discipline and effort. Challenge and opportunity lie along the same pathway. You are not going to elicit great change in the coaching structures of your club in a day, a week, a month or even a year. Depending on buy-in and skill set I see it as a process that will take at least five years to even near its potential. I must also note that well-meaning and diligent amateur coaches and clubs cannot be too hard on themselves. There will always be critics but once you are trying to better your situation in an honest manner you can take peace of mind from your work.

Finally, I hear some say *"This is all well and good but we have no coaches in our club"* It is my contention that for a club to be successful it must continually and actively recruit parents and up skill them as coaches. Target the parents. Make a role for them, up-skill them as best you can and you will soon have a happy and healthy coaching team and executive.

"Show me your coaches and I'll tell you your club."

Cohesive Collective Coaching is key.

Can you see?

CHAPTER 10
THE POWER OF THE CLUB
TO SERVE THE COMMUNITY

I won't go into huge detail here because there really should belittle need to. A question clubs must ask of themselves is; what is the long term purpose of our club? Invariably; at a superficial level it is to win at their given sport. Indeed, this is probably the 'sporting goal', but a club is so much more than just winning and losing and it cannot be defined as so. The long term purpose of the club is to serve the community and indeed society? The scope and potential of coaching and the power of 'Cohesive Collective Coaching' is just so vast.

Imagine if a club continually turned out happy, healthy, respectful children/adults of good character who shared a true friendship with each other. Wouldn't that locality be a great place to live? I would hazard a guess that this club would probably win a lot of games too because, as I am sure you can see, sporting success will always be the by-product of good coaching and a healthy sporting environment.

A final piece I like to mention to a club is that they should aim for 'conscious inclusiveness'. There is a role for everyone within a club. I often deal with parents of children with special needs and learning difficulties and they tell me with great sadness that they have nowhere to bring their child. If a club and its coaches have a created a healthy sporting environment it is beyond question that, within reason, every member of the community should be valued and given opportunities relative to their skill set. This not alone serves the child with difficulties, but also the other children as they learn to respect diversity and humanity. We will be producing well- rounded young people.

The power of the club to serve the community is enormous and far reaching. We must come to fully appreciate this and strive to develop our club structures to a level whereby we serve our community to the highest level. The club can have a truly higher purpose than the sport it represents. Its long term purpose must be to serve its community. Sporting success will simply happen as a consequence.

Serving the Community is key.

Can you see?

CHAPTER 11
THE END IS ALWAYS THE BEGINNING

"Genius is 1% inspiration and 99% perspiration"
Thomas Edison- Inventor

So you've reached the end, but as with almost everything in life, the end is always the beginning. I sincerely hope that you have enjoyed the book and found it thought provoking, challenging, and useful and that perhaps it will inspire the dawn of a new beginning in your coaching career. I hope it has helped you look at your role as coach with a new perspective and that that new perspective will lead to improvement. I hope it has helped to 'pull the coach out of you' and so you can go and 'pull the player out' of the children in front of you. I hope you now have an appreciation of how to challenge and assist them appropriately.

Be patient and have faith when coaching children. Impact doesn't happen in a moment. Be patient with both the children and yourself.

*"We are all apprentices in a craft where no one
ever becomes a master."*
Ernest Hemingway- Writer

Believe things will turn out as they should, provided you purposefully and consistently do what you should. Design the best practice session you can. Draw the player out. Consciously learn as you go. Invest in yourself and develop your craft. Have the patience to see success (your vision of it of course).

I have a fundamental belief in the power of coaching in child sport. I hope you can now fully appreciate the power of the Child Coach and that you have the potential to attain this power should you choose to pursue it. Use your lenses and this framework to build your 'coaching world'!

I will end with a little appeal; coach children well, give them the gift of a good start and as they leave childhood, be satisfied that you have played your part in bringing them to the end of their beginning in sport and not the beginning of the end. As adults, I believe it is our obligation to challenge and assist our young people appropriately. You can do this; at times you will doubt yourself but don't fall into the trap of selling yourself short. Go out and learn good coaching and enjoy the fruits of your labour. Learning is the essence of everything we do.

Best wishes Coach,

Paul Kilgannon

"Come to the edge," he said. "We can't, we're afraid!" they responded. "Come to the edge," he said. "We can't, we will fall!" they responded. "Come to the edge," he said. And so they came. And he pushed them. And they flew."

Guillaume Apollinaire- Poet, Playwright and Novelist

APPENDIX

Suggested Coaching Material

Books

- Mindset, by Carol Dweck, PhD.
- You Haven't Taught, Until They Have Learned, by John Wooden.
- Coaching Better Every Season, by Wade Gilbert.
- Coaching Science- Theory into Practice, by Terry McMorris and Tudor Hale.
- Nonlinear Pedagogy in Skill Acquisition- an introduction, by Chow, Davids, Button and Renshaw.
- Motor Learning in Practice- A Constraints – Led Approach, by Renshaw, Davids and Savelsbergh.
- The Sports Gene- Talent, Practice and The Truth About Success, by David Epstein.
- Pep Confidential, by Marti Perarnau.
- Play Practice- Second Edition- Engaging and Developing Skilled Players from Beginner to the Elite- by Alan Launder and Wendy Pitz.
- Athletic Development by Vern Gambetta.
- Athlete Centred Coaching by Lynn Kidman.

Podcasts

- The Perception and Action Podcast.
- The Talent Equation Podcast.
- Way of Champions Podcast.
- GAIN Cast.

KEY COACHING POINTS

Here are examples of KCP's of skills in various sports. When you know them you must come up with an effective way of coaching/ cueing them.

Striking from the hand in the game of Hurling

- This skill incorporates; throw, lock and swing.
- Throw the sliotar outwards from a cupped (catching) hand to below shoulder height.
- Move the catching hand to lock position.
- Step forward with the lead foot and swing the hurl downwards.
- Transfer the body weight onto the lead foot as the swing is completed.

Dribbling in Basketball
- Use fingertips, not the palms of hands.
- Legs soft, back straight, a low stance.
- Push the top of the ball down lightly by spreading the fingers and flexing the wrist and forearm.
- Don't look at the ball, head up and eyes forward, see with your fingertips.

Dribbling in Soccer
- Light touches on the ball keeping the ball close to your body (control).
- Use the inside and outside of right and your left foot.
- Head up so that you can see what's happening on the field.
- Lightly touch ball with foot each time you step forward alternating between right and left foot.

Running
- Posture–body in a neutral position!
- Arms Relaxed– full range of movement and not crossing body.
- Legs– the foot strike is from above, like a piston.

Session Plans

Below is a sample session for roughly 16 x nine-year-old boys in the game of hurling. This is not a perfect session (if such a thing exists) and is merely provided to give a **comprehensive example** of what a session plan might look like. I admit it is **very detail heavy** but again I am showing you every possible detail I have discussed in the planning session. Make and use of it what you will.

Children are to be bibbed into 4 teams of 4 as they arrive (this avoids needless timewasting). This sample session is planned with the understanding that the children have had previous experience and knowledge of this type of session lay out, the FMS games and the hurling skills and games. As a result, I have allowed for **absolute minimal transition and down times**.

After a full group socialising/ physical literacy warm up, the children are to be divided up into two groups of eight (2 of the pre picked teams x 2) under the guidance of two coaches. Groups alternate between 2a station and 2b station before moving on to 3a and 3b. The playzone and games based approaches are mixed. The session ends with a group FMS socialising game.

Possible weaknesses of the sample session are; that the hurling games are short and that we are trying to fit a large amount into the session. Again I am only doing this to give you a **comprehensive plan to study.**

Ideally we are looking for a 1 to 8 coach to child ratio. If you are head coach your job is to provide a structure that will facilitate the other coaches to contribute, use their skill set and add value to the session. Again nothing is perfect and you must adapt and overcome.

Sample Hurling Session- Under 9's- Date_____ Session Start Time- 7pm- Session Finish Time- 8pm

Values and Visions

- Your Why- To serve
- Your Values- REF
- Vision for Coach- Positively Different
- Your Coaching Team- CCC
- Vision for your players- Water
- Vision for your team- USA
- Vision for Success- A Smile

Broad Session Objectives

- Connect with every player
- Group is socialised
- Endorse Respect, Effort and Fun
- Challenge and assist to every child
- Purposefully address all pillars of the player

Age Related Considerations

- Focus on a mix of FMS and SSS

Targeted Skills

- Ground Swing
- Jab Lift

Coaching Techniques and Methodologies

- Games Based Approach
- Endorsing -Spot and raise Awareness-
- Coach by Contrast- Give them options A or B
- Coach by Questioning- Who, what, when, where, how, which, why???
- Direct Coaching if required
- Facilitate "Player to Player" Coaching

1- 7.00 pm- Whole Group Warm Up (SEE FMS GAMES)

a) Foxes and Hairs- MDSA
   - Time- 4 minutes
   - **Key Coaching Points/ RULES**

   Posture Arms Legs – PAL/ See FMS GAMES
   - **WILF**
   - Lots of the ABC'S/ "Tiny Feet"
   - **WALT**
   - Avoid contact in the game- Be quick!
   - **Resources, Numbers and Sizes**

   Cones and Bibs
   20m square playzone
   (1 minute transition)

b) Spellmaker- Frog, Bear, Ball etc. All FMS incorporated (SEE FMS GAMES)
   - Time- 3 mins
   - **Key Coaching Points**

   See FMS GAMES
   - **WILF**
   - Lots of FMS, relative strength body cohesion
   - **WALT**
   - Get Strong for hurling
   - **Resources, Numbers and Sizes**

   Cones and Bibs
   20m square playzone
   (4min transition to hurls, helmets and water)

c) Go through Hand Positions and Body Shapes of: Grip, Ready, Lock, Swing (left and right), pick, control, catch (2 mins)

   (1 minute transition)

2a 7.11 pm- Skill Based

The Ground Stroke/ Pull
- **Key Coaching Points**

Grip, Ready, Lock, Swing
Foot Position
- **WILF**

Movement in feet and foot positioning
Elbow out- Wrist action – C shape in the swing
Left and right
- **WALT**

Improve swing in ground hurling and this will transfer into striking from hand
- **Resources, Numbers and Sizes**

20m square playzone
Large sliotar and small sliotar- one of each per player

Practise technique without ball
- **Time- 1 minute**

Practise technique with ball- Random hitting in playzone- swing and find a new ball
- **Time- 2 minute**

Game – Bombs- Team A v Team B
- **Time- 3 x 2 minute games** (plus 30 sec reset x 2)

(1 minute transition)

2b 7.23- Games- Ground Hurling Only Game
- **Time-11 minutes total- 3 x 3 minute games** plus 30 sec reset x 2)
- **Key Coaching Points**

Grip, Ready, Lock, Swing
Foot Position
- **WILF**

Movement in feet and foot positioning
Elbow out- Wrist action - C shape in the swing
Left and right
- **WALT**

Move our feet and strike on the ground and this will transfer into all areas of the game
- **Resources, Numbers and Sizes**

Cones and 2 Goals- Pitch size 20m x 35m
Bibs 4 x 2 colours

In the games the challenge increases in a logical progression-

Game 1 - Conditions- Use big sliotar- one touch only
Game 2 - Conditions- Small sliotar- two touches (only if need)
Gaem 3 - Conditions- Small Sliotar- one touch only

(1 minute transition)

3a 7:35pm Skill Based- Jab Lift	3b 7:45 pm - Hurling Game	4 – 7:55 pm Whole Group End of Session FMS Game (SEE FMS GAMES)
Time-9 mins	**Time-9 mins**	Creepy Crawlers
Key Coaching Points	**Key Coaching Points**	➤ Time-3 mins (go second set up)
"Ready Position"- "hurl out" at the bottom	Principles of Game- Possession, Support	➤ **Key Coaching Points/ Rules**
Non-dominant hand is "on the tape" at the bottom		**SEE FMS GAMES**
Non- dominant foot beside the ball. Bend the knees and back- be "around the ball".	➤ **WILF**	➤ **WILF**
Hurl must be as parallel to the ground as possible.	Pick and Move (change shape/ direction)	• Teamwork
Catching Hand catches sliotar as low to the ground as possible.	➤ **WALT**	• Honesty
	Play the game and Gain Possession	➤ **WALT**
➤ **WILF**	➤ **Resources, Numbers and Sizes**	• Work as a team
Body shape of being "around the ball".		
➤ **WALT**	Cones and 2 Goals- Pitch size 20m x 35m	
Pick the ball- It is the number one performed skill in the game	Bibs 4 x 2 colours	Finish 8 o'clock
	Small Sliotars x 3	
➤ **Resources, Numbers and Sizes**		
	Scoring Options	
Layers- Progression and Regressions- Challenge increases in a logical progression	Goal 3 pts	
1. On knees	Point 1 pt	
2. Standing	First time ab lift 2pt	
3. Pick and drop move onto another		
4. How many in a minute	What gets measured and rewarded becomes important	
5. Pick and move with ball – 4 steps		
6. Pick and change direction and shape		
7. Pick and spin	(1 minute transition)	
8. Pick and move/ spin/ change direction and tap on hurl		
9. Contested		
Challenge- How many jab lifts in a minute x 3 –on rising the ball they must take four steps before dropping it and finding another ball		
(1 minute transition)		

Session Template - Team_____ - Date_____ Session Start Time_____ - Session Finish Time-_____

Values and Visions	Broad Session Objectives	Coaching Techniques and Methodologies
• Your Why- • Your Values- • Vision for Coach- • Your Coaching Team • Vision for your players- • Vision for your team- • Vision for Success-	**Age Related Considerations** **Targeted Skills**	• Games Based Approach • Endorsing • Spot and raise Awareness- • Coach by Contrast- Give them options A or B • Coach by Questioning- Who, what, when, where, how, which, why??? • Direct Coaching of KCPs can incorporate questioning style • Facilitate "Player to Player" Coaching

Time	Whole Group Warm Up	Time	Skill Based	Time	Games Based -
	a) Game/ Activity	Skill:		Game:-	
	Time:-				
	Key Coaching Points/ RULES	∆ Key Coaching Points		∆ Key Coaching Points	
	∆	∆		∆	
	WILF	WILF		WILF	
	∆	∆		∆	
	WALT	WALT		WALT	
	∆	∆		∆	
	Resources, Numbers and Sizes	Timing:-		Timing:-	
	∆	∆		∆	
	b) Game/ Activity	Resources, Numbers and Size		Resources, Numbers and Size	
	Timing:-	∆		∆	
	Key Coaching Points/ RULES				
	∆				
	WILF				
	∆				
	WALT				
	∆				
	Resources, Numbers and Sizes				
	∆				
	Transition Time_____	Transition Time_____		Transition Time_____	

Time _____ Skill Based	Time _____ Games Based _____	Whole Group End of Session FMS Game (SEE FMS GAMES)
Skill:	Game:	Game:
Key Coaching Points	Key Coaching Points	Key Coaching Points
▲	▲	▲
WILF	WILF	WILF
▲	▲	▲
WALT	WALT	WALT
▲	▲	▲
Timing:	Timing:	Timing:
▲	▲	▲
Resources, Numbers and Size	Resources, Numbers and Size	Resources, Numbers and Size
▲	▲	▲
Transition Time _____	Transition Time _____	Finish Time _____

Coaching System

Please take the time to read and reread the system. You will come to learn how simple yet effective it is. As the children get used to being coached through the system, their behaviour and attention will improve. As the sporting environment improves more 'real' coaching time will be available which can be used for the betterment of the child, the team and the club.

System 1- Sports Specific Skills and Physical Literacy /FMS Skills System in Play Zone.

8 Step Coaching System
1. Attention Getter- Sit/ kneel in a circle- Values REF.
2. Introduce skill and contextualise or connect skill to game- WALT.
3. Explain the skill using one or two key coaching points/ cues (minimal instruction- layer 1) or Coach by Comparison- WILF.
4. Agree Go and Pause signals/words.
5. Question to check understanding of skill and expectations.
6. Go signal/word.
7. Pause signal (word)- Coach/question/add layer or precision- Go signal (word). Repeat as needed.
8. End/debrief/question/appreciation.

Coaching System Explained
1. Attention Gatherer- Sit/kneel in a circle- Values REF

These are the tools the coach uses to gain the attention of the children at the beginning of the session or at any other time in the session the children are off task. They work!

Optional Attention Gatherer examples

1. Rhythmic Whistle Signal which the children will clap back e.g. 2 slow whistles, 3 fast. Repeat it a number of times. Vary it.

2. Match me- You do an action they copy. E.g. Hands on Head "Match Me", Hands on Shoulder's "Match Me". The only limiting factor is your imagination.
3. Mime the Skill- A set of mimes the children have been taught and know which practise the basic skill postures of the game while getting the children's attention e.g. "high catch", "low catch", etc.
4. "If you can hear my voice..." e.g. "run on the spot", "touch your toes". Can also be used to simulate any skill, teach body parts, etc.
5. Rhythm Clap- Coach leads a clapping pattern. Children replicate it.
6. Velcro Toes- Coach calls out the phrase "Velcro Toes" and all children know it means stand in a circle with toes touching the toes of the person either side of you.
7. Whistle Signals- Coach uses different pre agreed whistle signals to bring the children to order.

When you have their full attention bring them in together. You may only need to use this at the beginning of the session or after a break in activity

- Children are asked to sit/kneel in a semi-circle and then coach sits/kneels in front of them at their level. This is invaluable as children find it very difficult to stand still and look up at an adult. It also allows the coach to speak at your normal voice level (showing respect).
- The coach explains/refers to the motto/values of REF. "I expect three things; "Respect, Effort and Fun...Is that fair?", "I value effort not talent".

2. **Introduce Skill and Contextualise or Connect skill to game-WALT**

- E.g. "We are learning the Jab Lift" (hurling). This is the skill we use most to gain possession. Possession is the first principle of the game so I am sure you can see how important it is.

3. **Explain the skill using one or two KCPs/ cues or Coach by comparison- WILF**

- Keep instruction minimal. Look for one or 2 KCPs max. E.g. with jab lift for hurling it might be.
✓ Hurl flat to ground
✓ Lead foot beside the ball ('get around the ball')
  - If coaching by contrast- you could give two alternative options here.
  - Further layers will be added as the exercise develops. Raise awareness of precision.

4. **Agree a Go and Pause Signal/ Word**

- Example Go and Pause Signals- Go signal could be one whistle blow. Pause signal could be two whistle blows. If you want them to return to circle you do pause signal and then say "in and down".
- Example Go and Pause Words-Effective with younger children. Coach or children can choose them. Give the children a category and ask them to pick their favourites. Example, favourite player. Child A says "_____" Child B says "_____". Child A's choice is the Go word. Child B's choice is the Pause word.

5. **Question to check understanding of KCPS/WILF**

- Self-explanatory I hope

6. **Go Signal- Exercise**
   - The exercise begins with on the Go Signal or Word

7. **Pause Signal/Word- Coach/Question/Add layer or precision-Go Signal/Word- Repeat as needed**
   - This is the most important step. It is really the coaching step.
     1. You may wish to pause the exercise and 'add a layer', and recommence the exercise incorporating the improvements. Use the children as role models... "I love the way you side stepped, can you show us?" "Which is better Option A or B?"
     2. This pause step can be used multiple times to add multiple layers. You can pause and talk from their current positions or bring them in quickly, add the layer and get them out quickly.

8. **End/Debrief/Question/Appreciation**
   - End the exercise using a pause signal and "down and in" and the coach can endorse two or three points that they liked and one thing that can be improved. Pick various children for special mention. Promote the values and qualities you desire among your players. Question the children. Ask them what they've learned. Be patient with the reply.
   - Appreciation. Coach thanks the children; Children thank the coach.

System 2- FMS GAMES SYSTEM- 9 Step Coaching System

(Please note; much of this is the exact same as above but more specific to the FMS Games that follow.)

1. **Attention Gatherer- Sit/kneel in a circle- Values REF**
   As per system 1.

2. **Name the Game and get the children to repeat it.**
   (I will use a game call the Spell Maker which you will find later in the appendix. It is a great multi movement game for younger children).
   - "The name of the game we are going to play is "The Spell Maker". What's the name of the game?" Using repetition is a great way of engaging the children and keeping them on task.

3. **Learning Outcomes of the Game-Contextualise or Connect skill to game- WALT and WILF**
   - Explain the value of the activity through the language of athleticism and sportsmanship. It may be to develop a certain skill, physical quality (strength, agility, etc.) or it may develop non-physical qualities that will transfer to the sport or all of the above.
   - We want them to appreciate and understand what they are developing and why. We are teaching them about respect, friendship, leadership, communication, athleticism, etc. and we are creating healthy sporting environments. We want them to value these things.

4. **Explain the game- 3-4 basic guidelines**
   - Game Example, "In this game I am a Spell Maker who has the power to turn you into anything I wish. The game is played in the play zone. When I cast my spell you will act like that thing until I turn you into something else or back into yourself." I cast my spell by saying "I am the Spell Maker I am going to turn you into a _____" ...take

suggestions from the children (give the children a voice/input, create a healthy environment).

- <u>You don't have to over-coach the children at this stage.</u> Let them play the game as they see it. Let them make mistakes. The coaching will come after you observe what they do.

5. **Agree a Go and Pause Signal/Word**
As per system 1.

6. **Question to check understanding of game rules- WALT and WILF**
   - "Who am I... you are The Spell Maker", etc. (We are engaging the children and keeping them on task). What do you do? What do I expect?

7. **Go Signal or Word- Play Game**
   - The game begins with on the Go Signal or Word

8. **Pause Signal or Word/Coach/Question/Problem Solve**
This is the coaching step. You may wish to pause the game and,

   - ➢ Spot and raise awareness
   - ➢ Endorse
   - ➢ Coach by Comparison- Give them options A or B
   - ➢ Coach by Questioning- How can we change the game/ How can we improve it?
   - ➢ Coach directly when needed using cueing and KCP's

This "Pause" step can be used multiple times to add multiple layers. You can pause and talk from their current positions or bring them in quickly, add the layer and get them out quickly.

9. <u>**End/Debrief/Question/Appreciation**</u>
As per system 1.

CARVER Coach Reflection Log- Your Personal Total _____ (add the below together)

Area	1	2	3	4	5	6	7	8	9	10
I was well prepared; early, session plan complete and session set up.										
The session was fun. The children enjoyed it. I met their needs.										
I 'connected' with each player and actively socialised and connected the players in the team and the coaches.										
There was an appropriate blend of physical, technical, tactical and teamwork in my session.										
I treated them all relatively equally. I challenged each child appropriately; meeting them where they were at										
I raised awareness 'in game', 'of game and 'of self'. I coached through questioning and context										
My instruction was clear. I knew my coaching cues and KCP's										
I Endorsed well (REF, Principles of Game, Cues etc.).										
I promoted Healthy Living and Home Practice.										
I enjoyed my coaching today.										

I must start _____

I must stop _____

I must continue_____

What's Important Now (WIN)? _____

CARVER Player Reflection Log- Your Personal Total _____ (add the below together)

Rate your performance from 1 -10 in the following areas. 10 being excellent

Area	1	2	3	4	5	6	7	8	9	10
I enjoyed playing today										
I tried my best. I worked hard. I competed well										
My confidence was high										
I performed the skills of the game well										
My movement was good										
My decision making was good										
My support play with and without the ball was good										
I understood my role and what was expected of me										
My discipline was good I was a good team player										
I treated the referee and opposition with respect										

I must start _____

I must stop _____

I must continue_____

What's Important Now (WIN)? _____

Fundamental Movement Skills Games

Below you will find a small number of FMS Games that promote socialisation and Physical Literacy. I have picked up these games from multiple sources throughout the years. They can be used in warm ups, or in your FMS station in your session or at the end of the session. They are largely team based games which require team work and communication. You can teach lessons about sport and life through these games. Don't just play the games; raise the children's awareness of the value of these games. Explain what they are learning to do (WALT) and where it fits in and is connected with the game

Many and most of these games can be used with children from maybe 6 to 12 years old (indeed I often use them with adults) provided the playing and coaching environment is one of "Respect, Effort and Fun" REF. Remember that proper child coaching allows the child live out the fullness of their childhood.

Body Management Skills	Locomotor Skills	Object Control Skills
1. Rolling	1. Crawling	1. Throwing
2. Stopping	2. Running	2. Catching
3. Bending	3. Galloping	3. Striking
4. Twisting	4. Walking	4. Bouncing
5. Landing	5. Hopping	5. Dribbling
6. Stretching	6. Skipping	6. Kicking
7. Climbing	7. Dodging	
8. Balancing		
9. Turning		

I have broken the games into Body Weight Management Games and Locomotor Skills Games. I have purposely not included any Object Control Games. My reasoning behind this is that the vast majority of those reading the book will be child sports coaches and there will be a large amount of "object control" in the session already. Again I will remind you that relay races and target games are great ways to incorporate the skills of the game and blend them with the physical literacy activities. Through delivering the appropriate skill based challenges you should be addressing many of the "Object Control Skills."

Observation Model

A simple guide to observing the movement of a child;

- Feet- Mid foot ground contact in running. In avoiding contact, we are looking for agility- small steps. In shuffling and side stepping we want no crossing of legs.
- Knees- we want soft knees; especially on landing- "land soft"
- Hips- we want swagger in the hips
- Hands- moving freely and not crossing
- Posture- Upright- Head stable
- Face- Relaxed- ideally they are smiling :) Is there joy in the face?

Name of Game- The Spell Maker

- **FMS Category**- Locomotor Skills
- FMS prioritised within this game- All
- Linkage to other FMS- Body Management Skills

Sportsmanship skills and qualities- Promote and endorse the following;

- Information Processing
- Creativity and Self expression

Physical Skills and qualities- Promote and endorse the following;

- Body Control
- Precision

Materials and Equipment

- Cones

Activity Set up

- Play zone

Game Guidelines

- Coach is a magician and turns children into various objects/ things (animals, vehicles etc.).
- The children act like these objects until coach turns them into something else
- Coach says "I am the Spell Maker and I am going to turn you all into ..." e.g. aeroplanes, kangaroos, frogs, monkeys, motorbikes, footballs, pencils rolling around, snakes etc.

Adaptation

- Variety in the call will illicit different movements
- Assessment of learning/Questions for Children
- How does a _____ move?
- Which was the hardest most physically challenging movements?

Name of Game- Circle Switch

- **FMS Category-** Locomotor Skills
- FMS prioritised within this game- Running
- Linkage to other FMS – Body Management Skill

Sportsmanship skills and qualities- Promote and endorse the following;

- Information Processing- Non-verbal communication
- Team Work
- Tactical Awareness
- Decision Making

Physical Skills and qualities- Promote and endorse the following;

- Speed
- Agility

Materials and Equipment

- Cones
- Activity Set up
- Children stand in a large circle and place a cone under their legs.
- One child is "on" and stands in the middle of the circle at their cone.

Game Guidelines

- Children (12 minimum up to unlimited) must communicate their intention to switch places with another child in the circle. It must be a direct switch i.e. Child A must go to Child B's cone and B to A. It can't be child... A to B and B to D and C to B. A direct swop to each other's cone.
- Children swop places in this fashion. The circle should be a hive of activity
- If the child who is "on" gets to the free cone first during the switch, then the other child is now on
- Rock paper scissors used for conflict resolution

Adaptation

- Can use hop, crawl or skip movements
- Can incorporate carrying a ball or passing a ball
- Can condition it so that children can't talk i.e. create the need for non-verbal communication
  Assessment of learning/Questions for Children
- Why is peripheral vision important in sport?
- How can we change/ improve this game?

Name of Game- Everybody's On Tag

- **FMS Category-** Locomotor Skills
- FMS prioritised within this game- Running and Dodging
- Linkage to other FMS- Body Management Skills

Sportsmanship skills and qualities- Promote and endorse the following;

- Personal Responsibility- Honesty – Respect for the Game
- Physical Skills and qualities- Promote and Endorse the following;
- Speed
- Agility
- Evasion

Materials and Equipment

- Cones

Activity Set up

- Play zone

Game Guidelines

- Everybody is "on" i.e. everyone is a tagger until they get tagged
- Game starts and when you are tagged on the back you must kneel or lie on the ground. Tagging must be on the back between the shoulders
- The winner is the last person standing.
- To avoid a stand of at the end you can have 2 winners or use "rock, paper, scissors"

Adaptation

- Can incorporate ball as tagging object
- Assessment of learning/Questions for Children
- Why is bravery and courage important in sport (and life)?

Name of Game- Foxes and Hares

- **FMS Category-** Locomotor Skills
- FMS prioritised within this game- Running and Dodging
- Linkage to other FMS- Body management skills

Sportsmanship skills and qualities- Promote and endorse the following;

- Personal Responsibility- Respecting the Game

Physical Skills and qualities- Promote and endorse the following;

- Speed
- Agility
- Evasion

Materials and Equipment

- Cones
- Bibs- 1 per child

Activity Set up

- Play zone
- Children place bib into the back of their shorts

Game Guidelines

- Children place bib into the back of their shorts and leave the "tail" hanging long. These children are hares.
- One fox is picked.
- His job is to pull the tails from "The Hares".
- When a Hare loses its tail it becomes a fox until there is only one Hare left i.e. the winner
- Assessment of learning/Questions for Children
- Why are evasion skills important in sport?

Name of Game- Centipede March

- **FMS Category-** Locomotor Skills
- FMS prioritised within this game- Crawling
- **Linkage to other FMS-** Bodyweight management skills

Sportsmanship skills and qualities- Promote and endorse the following;

- Teamwork and Communication

Physical Skills and qualities- Promote and endorse the following;

- Body Control

Materials and Equipment

- Cones

Safety

- Mind children's knees on some surfaces

Activity Set up

- Point A to Point B

Game Guidelines

- Children are halfed- Approx. 5 on each team minimum
- Children get into a line on their hands and knees and link up by holding the ankles of the child in front i.e. creating a centipede
- The two 'centipedes' race each other in a crawling race from one point to another.
- If the line (centipede) breaks the team must call "Break" and 5 second "Penalty Stop" is imposed.

Adaptation

- Obstacle course can be incorporated
- Can be a one team timed based challenge
- Assessment of learning/Questions for Children
- What is important when people are working together?

Name of Game- Creepy Crawlers

- **FMS Category-** Locomotor Skills
- FMS prioritised within this game- Crawling
- Linkage to other FMS- Body Management Skills

Sportsmanship skills and qualities- Promote and endorse the following;

- Teamwork and Communication

Physical Skills and qualities- Promote and endorse the following;

- Body Control

Materials and Equipment

- Cones

Safety

- Mind children's knees on some surfaces

Activity Set up

- Point A to point B

Game Guidelines

- Group divided into teams of 5 minimum
- Each team stands in a line with their legs apart but toes touching.
- The child at the end of the line starts crawling in and out through the others' legs until they get to the top.
- The other children follow suit as they become last in the line and move the line along until the person you started at the top of the line gets back to their original place
- Game continues as so until team gets from Point A to Point B

Adaptation

- Can be a timed based challenge
- Can be a team based challenge
- Assessment of learning/Questions for Children
- What is important when people are working together

Name of Game-The Alphabet

- **FMS Category-** Body Management Skills
- FMS prioritised within this game- Balancing, Twisting, Stretching
- Linkage to other FMS- Locomotor Skills

Sportsmanship skills and qualities- Promote and endorse the following:

- Teamwork and Communication
- Creativity and Problem Solving

Physical Skills and qualities- Promote and endorse the following;

- Flexibility
- Good body control

Materials and Equipment

- Cones

Activity Set up

- Play zone

Game Guidelines

- Children run randomly around the play zone
- Coach calls out a number and a letter and children must form a group of this number and then, use various techniques to form the shape of that letter with their bodies.
- Coach calls out start word and children resume moving around until you call the next number and letter.
- Letters that are easier to form are: A, C, D, E, F, H, I, K, L, N, T, U, V, Y, Z
- Letters that are harder to form are: B, G, J, M, O, P, Q, R, S, W, X

Adaptation

- Use various locomotor skills between letters (e.g. skipping, hopping, running, jumping).
- Assessment of learning/Questions for Children
- What make a good team player?
- What can we do if someone is left out?

Name of Game- Cowboys and Indian Chief

- **FMS Category-** Body Management Skills
- FMS prioritised within this game- Non Specific
- Linkage to other FMS – Locomotor Skills

Sportsmanship skills and qualities- Promote and endorse the following;

- Teamwork, interpersonal skills and communication
- Creativity and Self expression

Physical Skills and qualities- Promote and endorse the following;

- Body Control

Materials and Equipment

- Cones

Activity Set up

- Play zone

Game Guidelines

- The group sits in a circle.
- One child (The Cowboy) is asked to leave the circle and turn away.
- An Indian Chief is picked.
- The Indian Chief leads the group in their own personal choice of claps, body movements or exercises. The group must follow the lead of the Indian Chief but try to keep their identity secret from the Cowboy who on returning has three guesses as to who the Indian Chief is.
- Adaptation- N/A
- Assessment of learning/Questions for kids
- Why is teamwork important in sport (and life)?
- What other exercises can we use?

Bibliography

Araújo, D. et al. (2019) 'Ecological cognition: expert decision-making behaviour in sport', International Review of Sport and Exercise Psychology.

Araújo, D., Davids, K. and Hristovski, R. (2006) 'The ecological dynamics of decision making in sport', Psychology of Sport and Exercise.

Barnett, L. M. et al. (2016) 'Fundamental movement skills: An important focus', Journal of Teaching in Physical Education.

Benz, A. et al. (2016) 'Coaching instructions and cues for enhancing sprint performance', Strength and Conditioning Journal.

Bernstein, N. A. (2020) 'Essay 5: Levels of Construction of Movements', in Dexterity and Its Development.

Bernstein, N. A., & Whyman, R. (1925). Biomechanics for Instructors. Moscow: Springer.

Bernstein, N. A., Latash, M. L., & Turvey, M. T. (n.d.). Dexterity and Its Development. Psychology Press.

Blandin, Y., Lhuisset, L. and Proteau, L. (1999) 'Cognitive Processes Underlying Observational Learning of Motor Skills', Quarterly Journal of Experimental Psychology Section A: Human Experimental Psychology.

Borg, G. A. V. (1973) 'Perceived exertion: A note on "history" and methods', Medicine and Science in Sports.

Bowers, E. P. et al. (2010) 'The Five Cs model of positive youth development: A longitudinal analysis of confirmatory factor structure and measurement invariance', Journal of Youth and Adolescence.

Burriss, K. and Burriss, L. (2011) 'Outdoor Play and Learning: Policy and Practice', International Journal of Education Policy and Leadership.

Camiré, M., Trudel, P. and Forneris, T. (2014) 'Examining how model youth sport coaches learn to facilitate positive youth development', Physical Education and Sport Pedagogy.

Castelli, D. M. et al. (2014) 'Physical literacy and Comprehensive School Physical Activity Programs', Preventive Medicine.

Chow, J. Y. et al. (2007) 'The role of nonlinear pedagogy in physical education', Review of Educational Research.

Chow, J. Y. (2015) Nonlinear Pedagogy in Skill Acquisition, Nonlinear Pedagogy in Skill Acquisition.

Clemente, F., Rocha, R. F. and Korgaokar, A. (2012) 'Teaching physical education: The usefulness of the teaching games for understanding and the constraints-led approach', Journal of Physical Education and Sport.

Correia, V. et al. (2019) 'Principles of nonlinear pedagogy in sport practice', Physical Education and Sport Pedagogy.

Côté, J. and Gilbert, W. (2009) 'An Integrative Definition of Coaching Effectiveness and Expertise', International Journal of Sports Science & Coaching.

Davids, K. et al. (2003) 'Acquiring skill in sport: a constraints led perspective', International Journal of Computer Science in Sport.

Davids, K. et al. (2012) 'Ecological dynamics and motor learning design in sport', in Skill Acquisition in Sport: Research, Theory and Practice.

Davids, K., Araújo, D., Vilar, L., et al. (2013) 'An ecological dynamics approach to skill acquisition: Implications for development of talent in sport', Talent Development and Excellence.

Davids, K., Araújo, D., Correia, V., et al. (2013) 'How small-sided and conditioned games enhance acquisition of movement and decision-making skills', Exercise and Sport Sciences Reviews.

Davids, K., Button, C. and Bennett, S. J. (2008) 'Dynamics of skill acquisition', Human Kinetics.

Davids, K. W., Button, C. and Bennett, S. J. (2008) 'Dynamics of Skill Acquisition: A Constraints-led', Human Kinetics.

den Duyn, N. Game sense: It's time to play. Sports Coach 19(4):9-11. 1997.

Dweck, C. S. (2009) 'Mindsets: Developing Talent Through a Growth Mindset', Olympic Coach.

Dweck S., C. (2015) 'Carol Dweck Revisits the "Growth Mindset"', Education Week.

Edwards, L. C. et al. (2017) 'Definitions, Foundations and Associations of Physical Literacy: A Systematic Review', Sports Medicine.

Edwards, L. C. et al. (2018) '"Measuring" Physical Literacy and Related Constructs: A Systematic Review of Empirical Findings', Sports Medicine.

Edwards, W. H. (2011) Motor Learning and Control: From Theory to Practice, SAS for Epidemiologists.

Eston, R. (2012) 'Use of ratings of perceived exertion in sports', International Journal of Sports Physiology and Performance.

Fajen, B. R., Riley, M. A. and Turvey, M. T. (2009) 'Information, affordances, and the control of action in sport', International Journal of Sport Psychology.

Gabbett, T. J. (2008) 'Do skill-based conditioning games offer a specific training stimulus for junior elite volleyball players?', Journal of Strength and Conditioning Research.

Gambetta, V. (2001) 'chapter 11: Incorporating Sport-Specific Skills into Conditioning: SOCCER.', in High-Performance Sports Conditioning.

Gamble, P. (2004) 'A skill-based conditioning games approach to metabolic conditioning for elite rugby football players', Journal of Strength and Conditioning Research.

Giblin, S., Collins, D. and Button, C. (2014) 'Physical literacy: Importance, assessment and future directions', Sports Medicine.

Gilbert, W. D. and Trudel, P. (2001) 'Learning to coach through experience: Reflection in model youth sport coaches', Journal of Teaching in Physical Education.

Gilbert, W. D. and Trudel, P. (2005) 'Learning to coach through experience: Conditions that influence reflection', The Physical Educator.

Gréhaigne, J. F. and Godbout, P. (2014) 'Dynamic Systems Theory and Team Sport Coaching', Quest.

Güllich, A. (2017) 'International medallists' and non-medallists' developmental sport activities–a matched-pairs analysis', Journal of Sports Sciences.

Halliwell, B. et al. (2017) 'The Effects of Growth Mindset Intervention on Vocabulary Skills in First to Third Grade Children', Academic Festival.

Halperin, I. et al. (2016) 'Coaching cues in amateur boxing: An analysis of ringside feedback provided between rounds of competition', Psychology of Sport and Exercise.

Hardy, L. L. et al. (2010) 'Fundamental movement skills among Australian preschool children', Journal of Science and Medicine in Sport.

Harrison, A. J. (2010) 'BIOMECHANICAL FACTORS IN SPRINT TRAINING-WHERE SCIENCE MEETS COACHING .', Biomechanics.

Hedges, H. and Cooper, M. (2018) 'Relational play-based pedagogy: theorising a core practice in early childhood education', Teachers and Teaching: Theory and Practice.

Helsen, W. F., Starkes, J. L. and Hodges, N. J. (1998) 'Team sports and the theory of deliberate practice', Journal of Sport and Exercise Psychology.

Holfelder, B. and Schott, N. (2014) 'Relationship of fundamental movement skills and physical activity in children and adolescents: A systematic review', Psychology of Sport and Exercise.

Hopper, T. (1998) 'Teaching games for understanding using progressive principles of play', CAHPERD.

Iacovides, I. et al. (2011) 'Making sense of game-play: How can we examine learning and involvement?', in Proceedings of DiGRA 2011 Conference: Think Design Play.

Jurbala, P. (2015) 'What Is Physical Literacy, Really?', Quest.

Kee, Y. H. (2019) 'Reflections on athletes' mindfulness skills development: Fitts and Posner's (1967) three stages of learning', Journal of Sport Psychology in Action.

Lawson, E. Incorporating sport-specific drills into conditioning. In: High-Performance Sports Conditioning. B. Foran, ed. Champaign, IL: Human Kinetics, 2001. pp. 215-266.

Leahey, S., 2012. The science & application of coaching cues. Retrieved from. 2012

Lewkowicz, D. J. and Lickliter, R. (1995) 'A Dynamic Systems Approach to the Development of Cognition and Action', Journal of Cognitive Neuroscience.

Lhuisset, L. and Margnes, E. (2015) 'The influence of live- vs. video-model presentation on the early acquisition of a new complex coordination', Physical Education and Sport Pedagogy.

Lloyd, R. S. et al. (2015) 'Long-term athletic development- Part 1: A pathway for all youth', Journal of Strength and Conditioning Research.

Lloyd, R. S. and Oliver, J. L. (2012) 'The youth physical development model: A new approach to long-term athletic development', Strength and Conditioning Journal.

Lubans, D. R. et al. (2010) 'Fundamental Movement Skills in Children and Adolescents', Sports Medicine.

Lundvall, S. (2015) 'Physical literacy in the field of physical education - A challenge and a possibility', Journal of Sport and Health Science.

Le Magueresse-Battistoni, B. (2007) 'Serine proteases and serine protease inhibitors in testicular physiology: The plasminogen activation system', Reproduction.

Massey, S. L. (2013) 'From the Reading Rug to the Play Center: Enhancing Vocabulary and Comprehensive Language Skills by Connecting Storybook Reading and Guided Play', Early Childhood Education Journal.

Masters, G. N. (2006) 'Towards a growth mindset in assessment', Practically Primary.

McMahon, E. M. et al. (2017) 'Physical activity in European adolescents and associations with anxiety, depression and well-being', European Child and Adolescent Psychiatry.

Moy, B., Renshaw, I. and Davids, K. (2016) 'The impact of nonlinear pedagogy on physical education teacher education students' intrinsic motivation', Physical Education and Sport Pedagogy.

Muyor, J. M. (2013) 'Exercise intensity and validity of the ratings of perceived exertion (Borg and OMNI Scales) in an indoor cycling session', Journal of Human Kinetics.

Nelson, L. J. and Cushion, C. J. (2006) 'Reflection in coach education: The case of the national governing body coaching certificate', in Sport Psychologist.

Okely, A. D., Booth, M. L. and Patterson, J. W. (2001) 'Relationship of physical activity to fundamental movement skills among adolescents', Medicine and Science in Sports and Exercise.

Parker, M. B. and Curtner-Smith, M. (2005) 'Health-related fitness in sport education and multi-activity teaching', Physical Education & Sport Pedagogy.

Physical, T. and Tools, L. (2014) 'Physical Literacy Assessment in Canada', Physical & Health Education Journal.

Pill, S., & Drummond, M. (2016). Game Sense Coaching: Developing Thinking Players.

Popović, B. et al. (2020) 'Evaluation of gross motor coordination and physical fitness in children: Comparison between soccer and multisport activities', International Journal of Environmental Research and Public Health.

Potgieter, R. and Steyn, B. (2013) 'Goal orientation, self-theories and reactions to success and failures in competitive sport', African Journal for Physical, Health Education, Recreation and Dance.

Renshaw, I. et al. (2010) 'A constraints-led perspective to understanding skill acquisition and game play: A basis for integration of motor learning theory and physical education praxis?', Physical Education and Sport Pedagogy.

Renshaw, I., Davids, K. and Savelsbergh, G. J. P. (2010) Motor learning in practice: A constraints-led approach, Motor Learning in Practice: A Constraints-Led Approach.

De Rugy, A. et al. (2002) 'Perception - Action coupling model for human locomotor pointing', Biological Cybernetics.

Scherr, J. et al. (2013) 'Associations between Borg's rating of perceived exertion and physiological measures of exercise intensity', European Journal of Applied Physiology.

'Shared affordances guide interpersonal synergies in sport teams' (2020) in Interpersonal Coordination and Performance in Social Systems.

Silva, P. et al. (2013) 'Shared knowledge or shared affordances? insights from an ecological dynamics approach to team coordination in sports', Sports Medicine.

Smith, L. B. and Thelen, E. (2003) 'Development as a dynamic system', Trends in Cognitive Sciences.

Starkes, J. L. et al. (1996) 'Deliberate practice in sports: What is it anyway?', in The road to excellence: The acquisition of expert performance in the arts and sciences, sports, and games.

Stone, M. H., Stone, M. and Sands, W. A. (2007) Principles and Practice of Resistance Training, Principles and Practice of Resistance Training.

Tenison, C. and Anderson, J. R. (2016) 'Modeling the distinct phases of skill acquisition', Journal of Experimental Psychology: Learning Memory and Cognition.

Thelen, E. and Smith, L. B. (2007) 'Dynamic Systems Theories', in Handbook of Child Psychology.

Vierimaa, M. et al. (2012) 'Positive youth development: A measurement framework for sport', International Journal of Sports Science and Coaching. d

Visek, A. J. et al. (2015) 'The fun integration theory: Toward sustaining children and adolescents sport participation', Journal of Physical Activity and Health.

Visual Perception and Action in Sport (2005) Visual Perception and Action in Sport.

Weinbauer, G. F. et al. (2010) 'Physiology of testicular function', in Andrology: Male Reproductive Health and Dysfunction.

Whitehead, M. (2010) Physical literacy: Throughout the lifecourse, Physical Literacy: Throughout the Lifecourse.

ABOUT THE AUTHOR

Paul Kilgannon is a primary school teacher, sports coach and coach educator from Galway, Ireland. He has coached children, teens and adults throughout his adult life. This book is the culmination of his work in sport and education and is designed for coaches who wish to make a positive difference to the lives of children, enjoy their coaching and develop as a coach. The CARVER Framework is a set of highly usable lenses and tools for the coach in team sport. This is a book about learning and practice. Continuous learning is the job, and indeed the art, of coaching. This book is designed to assist you in building your 'Coaching World'. This is....

"Not another book of drills"

CPSIA information can be obtained
at www.ICGtesting.com
Printed in the USA
LVHW102112131122
733056LV00005B/117